William Shakespeare's

ROMEO AND JULIET

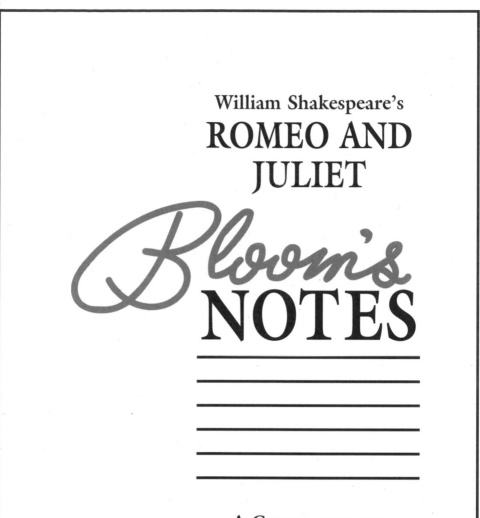

NOTES

A CONTEMPORARY
LITERARY VIEWS BOOK

Edited and with an Introduction by
HAROLD BLOOM

3 5 7 9 8 6 4

Cover illustration: Photofest

Library of Congress Cataloging-in-Publication Data

William Shakespeare's Romeo and Juliet / Harold Bloom, editor.
p.   cm. — (Bloom's Notes)
"Books by William Shakespeare":
Includes bibliographical references and index.
Summary: Includes a brief biography of William Shakespeare, thematic and structural analysis of the work, critical views, and an index of themes and ideas.
ISBN 0-7910-3671-5
1. Shakespeare, William, 1564–1616. Romeo and Juliet. 2. Tragedy.
[1. Shakespeare, William, 1564–1616. Romeo and Juliet. 2. English literature—History and criticism.] I. Bloom, Harold. II. Series.
PR2831.W55 1995
822.3'3—dc20
95-23726
CIP
AC

Chelsea House Publishers
1974 Sproul Road, Suite 400
P.O. Box 914
Broomall, PA 19008-0914

Contents

User's Guide

This volume is designed to present biographical, critical, and bibliographical information on William Shakespeare and *Romeo and Juliet.* Following Harold Bloom's introduction, there appears a detailed biography of the author, discussing the major events in his life and his important literary works. Then follows a thematic and structural analysis of the work, in which significant themes, patterns, and motifs are traced. An annotated list of characters supplies brief information on the chief characters in the work.

A selection of critical extracts, derived from previously published material by leading critics, then follows. The extracts consist of statements by the author on his work, early notices of the work, and later evaluations down to the present day. The items are arranged chronologically by date of first publication. A bibliography of Shakespeare's writings (including a complete listing of all books he wrote, cowrote, edited, and translated, and selected posthumous publications), a list of additional books and articles on him and on *Romeo and Juliet,* and an index of themes and ideas conclude the volume.

Harold Bloom is Sterling Professor of the Humanities at Yale University and Henry W. and Albert A. Berg Professor of English at the New York University Graduate School. He is the author of twenty books and the editor of more than thirty anthologies of literature and literary criticism.

Professor Bloom's works include *Shelley's Mythmaking* (1959), *The Visionary Company* (1961), *Blake's Apocalypse* (1963), *Yeats* (1970), *A Map of Misreading* (1975), *Kabbalah and Criticism* (1975), and *Agon: Towards a Theory of Revisionism* (1982). *The Anxiety of Influence* (1973) sets forth Professor Bloom's provocative theory of the literary relationships between the great writers and their predecessors. His most recent books are *The American Religion* (1992) and *The Western Canon* (1994).

Professor Bloom earned his Ph.D. from Yale University in 1955 and has served on the Yale faculty since then. He is a 1985 MacArthur Foundation Award recipient and served as the Charles Eliot Norton Professor of Poetry at Harvard University in 1987–88. He is currently the editor of the Chelsea House series Major Literary Characters and Modern Critical Views, and other Chelsea House series in literary criticism.

Introduction

HAROLD BLOOM

Harold C. Goddard, in his *The Meaning of Shakespeare* (1951), remarked upon how much of Shakespeare turns upon the vexed relationships between generations of the same family, which was also one of the burdens of Athenian tragedy. Except for the early *Titus Andronicus,* which I judge to have been a charnel-house parody of Christopher Marlowe, *Romeo and Juliet* was Shakespeare's first venture at composing a tragedy, and also his first deep investigation of generational perplexities. The Montague-Capulet hatred might seem overwrought enough to have its parodistic aspects, but it destroys two immensely valuable, very young lovers, Juliet of the Capulets and Romeo of the Montagues, and Mercutio as well, a far more interesting character than Romeo. Yet Romeo, exalted by the authentic love between the even more vital Juliet and himself, is one of the first instances of the Shakespearean representation of crucial change in a character through self-overhearing and self-reflection. Juliet, an even larger instance, is the play's triumph, since she inaugurates Shakespeare's extraordinary procession of vibrant, life-enhancing women, never matched before or since in all of Western literature, including in Chaucer, who was Shakespeare's truest precursor as the creator of personalities.

Juliet, Mercutio, the nurse, and to a lesser extent Romeo are among the first Shakespearean characters who manifest their author's uncanny genius at inventing persons. Richard III, like Aaron the Moor in *Titus Andronicus,* is a brilliant Marlovian cartoon or grotesque, but lacks all inwardness, which is true also of the figures in the earliest comedies. Faulconbridge the Bastard in *King John* and Richard II were Shakespeare's initial breakthroughs in the forging of personalities, before the composition of *Romeo and Juliet.* After Juliet, Mercutio, and the nurse came Bottom, Shylock, Portia, and most overwhelmingly Falstaff, with whom at last Shakespeare was fully himself. Harold Goddard shrewdly points out that the nurse, who lacks wit, imagination, and above all love, even for Juliet, is no

Falstaff, who abounds in cognitive power, creative humor, and (alas) love for the undeserving Hal. The nurse is ferociously lively and funny, but she proves to be exactly what the supremely accurate Juliet eventually calls her: "most wicked fiend," whose care for Juliet has no inward reality. In some sense, the agent of Juliet's tragedy is the nurse, whose failure in loving the child she has raised leads Juliet to the desperate expedient that destroys both Romeo and herself.

Mercutio, a superb and delightful role, nevertheless is inwardly quite as cold as the nurse. Though he is Shakespeare's first sketch of a charismatic individual (Berowne in *Love's Labor's Lost* has brilliant language, but no charisma), Mercutio is a dangerous companion for Romeo, and becomes redundant as soon as Romeo passes from sexual infatuation to sincere love, from Rosaline to Juliet. Age-old directorial wisdom is that Shakespeare killed off Mercutio so quickly, because Romeo is a mere stick in contrast to his exuberant friend. But Mercutio becomes irrelevant once Juliet and Romeo fall profoundly in love with one another. What place has Mercutio in the play once it becomes dominated by Juliet's magnificent avowal of her love's infinitude:

> And yet I wish but for the thing I have.
> My bounty is as boundless as the sea,
> My love as deep; the more I give to thee,
> The more I have, for both are infinite.

Contrast that with Mercutio at his usual bawdry:

> If love be blind, love cannot hit the mark.
> Now will he sit under a medlar tree,
> And wish his mistress were that kind of fruit
> As maids call medlars, when they laugh alone.
> O, Romeo, that she were, O that she were
> An open-arse, thou a pu'rin pear!

Since Juliet develops from strength to strength, Romeo (who is only partly a convert to love) is inevitably dwarfed by her. Partly this is the consequence of what will be Shakespeare's long career of comparing women to men to men's accurate disadvantage, a career that can be said to commence with precisely this play. But partly the tragic flaw is in Romeo himself, who yields too readily to many fierce emotions: anger, fear, grief, despair. This yielding leads to the death of Tybalt, to Romeo's own suicide, and to Juliet's own farewell to life. Shakespeare is careful to make Romeo just as culpable, in his way, as Mercutio or Tybalt. Juliet, in total contrast, remains radically free of flaw: she is a saint of love, courageous and trusting, refusing the nurse's evil counsel and attempting to hold on to love's truth, which she incarnates. Though it is "The Tragedy of Romeo and Juliet," the lovers are tragic in wholly different ways. Juliet, in a curious prophecy of Hamlet's charismatic elevation, transcends her self-destruction and dies exalted. Romeo, not of her eminence, dies more pathetically. We are moved by both deaths, but Shakespeare sees to it that our larger loss is the loss of Juliet. ❖

Biography of
William Shakespeare

Few events in the life of William Shakespeare are supported by reliable evidence, and many incidents recorded by commentators of the last four centuries are either conjectural or apocryphal.

William Shakespeare was born in Stratford-upon-Avon on April 22 or 23, 1564, the son of Mary Arden and John Shakespeare, a tradesman. His very early education was in the hands of a tutor, for his parents were probably illiterate. At age seven he entered the Free School in Stratford, where he learned the "small Latin and less Greek" attributed to him by Ben Jonson. When not in school Shakespeare may have gone to the popular Stratford fairs and to the dramas and mystery plays performed by traveling actors.

When Shakespeare was about thirteen his father removed him from school and apprenticed him to a butcher, although it is not known how long he remained in this occupation. When he was eighteen he married Anne Hathaway; their first child, Susanna, was born six months later. A pair of twins, Hamnet and Judith, were born in February 1585. About this time Shakespeare was caught poaching deer on the estate of Sir Thomas Lucy of Charlecot; Lucy's prosecution is said to have inspired Shakespeare to write his earliest literary work, a satire on his opponent. Shakespeare was convicted of poaching and forced to leave Stratford. He withdrew to London, leaving his family behind. He soon attached himself to the stage, initially in a menial capacity (as tender of playgoers' horses, according to one tradition), then as prompter's attendant. When the poaching furor subsided, Shakespeare returned to Stratford to join one of the many bands of itinerant actors. In the next five years he gained what little theatre training he received.

By 1592 Shakespeare was a recognized actor, and in that year he wrote and produced his first play, *Henry VI, Part One.* Its success impelled Shakespeare soon afterward to write the second and third parts of *Henry VI.* (Many early and modern critics believed that *Love's Labour's Lost* preceded these histories as Shakespeare's earliest play, but the majority of modern scholars discount this theory.) Shakespeare's popularity provoked the jealousy of Robert Greene, as recorded in his posthumous *Groats-worth of Wit* (1592).

In 1593 Shakespeare published *Venus and Adonis,* a long poem based upon Ovid (or perhaps upon Arthur Golding's translation of Ovid's *Metamorphoses*). It was dedicated to the young earl of Southampton—but perhaps without permission, a possible indication that Shakespeare was trying to gain the nobleman's patronage. However, the dedicatory address to Southampton in the poem *The Rape of Lucrece* (1594) reveals Shakespeare to have been on good terms with him. Many plays—such as *Titus Andronicus, The Comedy of Errors,* and *Romeo and Juliet*—were produced over the next several years, most performed by Shakespeare's troupe, the Lord Chamberlain's Company. In December 1594 Shakespeare acted in a comedy (of unknown authorship) before Queen Elizabeth; many other royal performances followed in the next decade.

In August 1596 Shakespeare's son Hamnet died. Early the next year Shakespeare bought a home, New Place, in the center of Stratford; he is said to have planted a mulberry tree in the backyard with his own hands. Shakespeare's relative prosperity is indicated by his purchasing more than a hundred acres of farmland in 1602, a cottage near his estate later that year, and half-interest in the tithes of some local villages in 1605.

In September 1598 Shakespeare began his friendship with the then unknown Ben Jonson by producing his play *Every Man in His Humour.* The next year the publisher William Jaggard affixed Shakespeare's name, without his permission, to a curious medley of poems under the title *The Passionate Pilgrim;* the majority of the poems were not by Shakespeare. Two of his sonnets, however, appeared in this collection, although the 154 sonnets, with their mysterious dedication to "Mr. W. H.," were not published as a group until 1609. Also in 1599 the Globe Theatre was built in Southwark (an area of London), and Shakespeare's company began acting there. Many of his greatest plays—*Troilus and Cressida, King Lear, Othello, Macbeth*—

were performed in the Globe before its destruction by fire in 1613.

The death in 1603 of Queen Elizabeth, the last of the Tudors, and the accession of James I, from the Stuart dynasty of Scotland, created anxiety throughout England. Shakespeare's fortunes, however, were unaffected, as the new monarch extended the license of Shakespeare's company to perform at the Globe. James I saw a performance of *Othello* at the court in November 1604. In October 1605 Shakespeare's company performed before the Mayor and Corporation of Oxford.

The last five years of Shakespeare's life seem void of incident; he had retired from the stage by 1613. Among the few known incidents is Shakespeare's involvement in a heated and lengthy dispute about the enclosure of common-fields around Stratford. He died on April 23, 1616, and was buried in the Church of St. Mary's in Stratford. A monument was later erected to him in the Poets' Corner of Westminster Abbey.

Numerous corrupt quarto editions of Shakespeare's plays were published during his lifetime. These editions, based either on manuscripts, promptbooks, or sometimes merely actors' recollections of the plays, were meant to capitalize on Shakespeare's renown. Other plays, now deemed wholly or largely spurious—*Edward III, The Yorkshire Tragedy, The Two Noble Kinsmen,* and others—were also published under Shakespeare's name during and after his lifetime. Shakespeare's plays were collected in the First Folio of 1623 by John Heminge and Henry Condell. Nine years later the Second Folio was published, and in 1640 Shakespeare's poems were collected. The first standard collected edition was by Nicholas Rowe (1709), followed by the editions of Alexander Pope (1725), Lewis Theobald (1733), Samuel Johnson (1765), Edmond Malone (1790), and many others.

Shakespeare's plays are now customarily divided into the following categories (probable dates of writing are given in brackets): comedies (*The Comedy of Errors* [1590], *The Taming of the Shrew* [1592], *The Two Gentlemen of Verona* [1592–93], *A Midsummer Night's Dream* [1595], *Love's Labour's Lost* [1595], *The Merchant of Venice* [1596–98], *As You Like It*

[1597], *The Merry Wives of Windsor* [1597], *Much Ado About Nothing* [1598–99], *Twelfth Night* [1601], *All's Well That Ends Well* [1603–04], and *Measure for Measure* [1604]); histories (*Henry VI, Part One* [1590–92], *Henry VI, Parts Two and Three* [1590–92], *Richard III* [1591], *King John* [1591–98], *Richard II* [1595], *Henry IV, Part One* [1597], *Henry IV, Part Two* [1597], *Henry V* [1599], and *Henry VIII* [1613]); tragedies (*Titus Andronicus* [1590], *Romeo and Juliet* [1595], *Julius Caesar* [1599], *Hamlet* [1599–1601], *Troilus and Cressida* [1602], *Othello* [1602–04], *King Lear* [1604–05], *Macbeth* [1606], *Timon of Athens* [1607], *Antony and Cleopatra* [1606–07], and *Coriolanus* [1608]); romances (*Pericles, Prince of Tyre* [1606–08], *Cymbeline* [1609–10], *The Winter's Tale* [1610–11], and *The Tempest* [1611]). However, Shakespeare willfully defied the canons of classical drama by mingling comedy, tragedy, and history, so that in some cases classification is debatable or arbitrary.

Shakespeare's reputation, while subject to many fluctuations, was firmly established by the eighteenth century. Samuel Johnson remarked: "Perhaps it would not be easy to find any authour, except Homer, who invented so much as Shakespeare, who so much advanced the studies which he cultivated, who effused so much novelty upon his age or country. The form, the characters, the language, and the shows of the English drama are his." Early in the nineteenth century Samuel Taylor Coleridge declared: "The Englishman who without reverence, a proud and affectionate reverence, can utter the name of William Shakespeare, stands disqualified for the office of critic. . . . Great as was the genius of Shakespeare, his judgment was at least equal to it."

A curious controversy developed in the middle of the nineteenth century in regard to the authorship of Shakespeare's plays, some contending that Sir Francis Bacon was the actual author of the plays, others (including Mark Twain) advancing the claims of the earl of Oxford. None of these attempts has succeeded in persuading the majority of scholars that Shakespeare himself is not the author of the plays attributed to him.

In recent years many landmark editions of Shakespeare, with increasingly accurate texts and astute critical commentary, have emerged. These include *The Arden Shakespeare* (1951–), *The Oxford Shakespeare* (1982–), and *The New Cambridge Shakespeare* (1984–). Such critics as T. S. Eliot, G. Wilson Knight, Northrop Frye, W. H. Auden, and many others have continued to elucidate Shakespeare, his work, and his times, and he remains the most written-about author in the history of English literature. ❖

Thematic and Structural Analysis

The Tragedy of Romeo and Juliet begins with the appearance of the chorus, who introduces the work with a **prologue** in the form of a sonnet. The prologue informs the audience that this play is about two wealthy families in the city of Verona, Italy (the date is unspecified), who are engaged in a bitter feud. A son and a daughter from the two families fall in love, meet with ill fortune, commit suicide, and "with their death bury their parents' strife." The sad story line is repeated, and the chorus apologizes in advance for any deficiencies in the performance.

The violence and the persistence of the Montague-Capulet feud, emphasized by the prologue, is immediately demonstrated in **Act I, scene 1** of the play. Two servants of the Capulets, Sampson and Gregory, walk through the streets of Verona armed with swords and small shields. In their conversation it becomes clear that they are seeking to brawl with some Montagues. Their motivation seems somewhat vague, and their conversation is pugnacious and vulgar; Sampson in particular brags that he will beat all the Montague men and rape all the Montague women.

This boasting is promptly put to the test with the arrival upon the scene of two servants of the house of Montague, Abram and Balthasar, the latter being Romeo's personal servant. Gregory and Sampson confer as to how to provoke a brawl while staying on the right side of Verona's laws, which forbid fighting or provoking fights in the streets. Sampson bites his thumb at Abram and Balthasar (a gesture of extreme disdain). But when Abram challenges Sampson, asking, "Do you bite your thumb at us, sir?" Gregory informs Sampson that replying yes would be breaking the law, and Sampson is placed in the ridiculous position of claiming that while he did indeed bite his thumb, the gesture was not made toward anybody in particular.

Not surprisingly, Sampson's disclaimer does little to pacify Abram, who challenges him to claim that he is the better man. At this point Benvolio, a member of the Montague family, enters the scene and is spied by Gregory. Gregory, assuming that Benvolio will protect them or be impressed by their fighting, tells the faltering Sampson to say that he is better than Abram; Sampson does, and the servants attack each other. Benvolio, far from encouraging the fight, forcefully breaks it up by beating down the servants' swords with his own. He is spotted in his efforts by the hotheaded Tybalt, a Capulet and Juliet's mother's nephew, who accuses Benvolio of attacking the servants. When Benvolio claims he was only trying to make peace, Tybalt sums up his own character by retorting, "I hate the word / As I hate hell, all Montagues, and thee," and attacks the hapless Benvolio.

The fight attracts a few fed-up Verona citizens, who, in addition to breaking up the fight with a variety of blunt instruments, cry out their disapproval of the feud: "Down with the Capulets! Down with the Montagues!" The elderly patriarch of the Capulets appears with his wife and promptly demands a sword when he sees the similarly decrepit head of the Montagues, who has also been attracted by the scene. The two men are easily prevented from fighting by their wives until the prince of Verona, Escalus, enters and soundly chastises the two men for allowing their conflict ("bred of an airy word," according to Escalus) to break out repeatedly in the city. "If ever you disturb our streets again," Escalus warns the two men, "your lives shall pay the forfeit of the peace."

The prince leaves with old Capulet, promising to see Montague that afternoon, and the crowd disperses, leaving Montague, Lady Montague, and Benvolio. The Montagues ask Benvolio to describe how the fight began, but the conversation soon turns to the whereabouts of their son Romeo, who has been moody and withdrawn lately for unknown reasons. The topic of their conversation handily appears, and Benvolio bids the Montagues to depart so that he can query Romeo as to the cause of his sadness.

Benvolio does not wonder long, for Romeo readily reveals that he is in love and that the woman he loves—Rosaline—does not return his favor. Romeo's bewailing of his fate is, to say the least, self-indulgent—he interrupts his own request for an account of the recent brawl in order to continue bemoaning his plight. He speaks in elevated rhymed couplets, and his language is filled with apostrophes and similes. Although sympathetic, Benvolio obviously has a hard time taking Romeo's passion seriously; he rather cynically suggests that Romeo can cure his love by simply meeting other pretty ladies and comparing Rosaline's none-too-exceptional face to theirs.

Act I, scene 2 takes the reader to the Capulets and another sort of love. Old Capulet, accompanied by a servant, is discussing his recent chastisement by the prince with County (Count) Paris, a young nobleman who is kin to Prince Escalus (and thus of higher social rank than the Capulets). Paris quickly changes the topic of conversation: He has asked for the hand of Juliet, Capulet's daughter, and wishes for a response. Capulet objects that Juliet is too young to marry. He also indicates that he is favorably inclined to the suit but that he will defer to Juliet's wish.

The back-to-back scenes with Romeo and with Paris serve a number of purposes in the play. First, there is the inevitable establishment of barriers to the couple's romance (the "right" couple—Romeo and Juliet—having been established in both the play's title and its prologue) that will just as inevitably be overcome later on in the play. In addition, there is the presentation in these scenes of a number of false loves—Romeo's juvenile love for Rosaline, Capulet's hypocritical statement of concern for Juliet that simply masks a deeper love of money and position, and Paris's seemingly sincere but totally unrequited love for Juliet. These loves (especially the first two) seem to serve as a foil to Romeo and Juliet's later love; although it can be argued that their love is impulsive and ill advised, it is decidedly more attractive to the audience than Romeo's whining or Capulet's unscrupulousness. Such implicit contrasts reoccur throughout the play.

Capulet's interest in marrying his daughter to Paris becomes evident when he invites the count to a party at his house that evening. The two go off to confer, leaving Capulet's servant with a list of people to invite. The servant, however, is illiterate and decides to find an educated person to decipher the list for him. Just then, Benvolio and Romeo appear, still arguing over whether or not Romeo can cure his passion for Rosaline by meeting other women. The servant asks them to read the list for him, and when they do he repays the favor by inviting them to the Capulets' party (provided that they are not of the house of Montague, of course). The list of guests included Rosaline and a number of other young women; Benvolio points out that this is an excellent opportunity for Romeo to see other beauties and realize that Rosaline is only one of many. Romeo disagrees with this contention but agrees to go anyway in order to see his love.

Act I, scene 3 unfolds in the Capulet household, where Lady Capulet, Juliet, and Juliet's nurse are engaged in a serious discussion. At first, they attempt to determine exactly how old Juliet is, and the nurse quickly reveals herself to be somewhat addlepated and overly talkative; nonetheless she is obviously quite fond of Juliet and is a trusted family confidante in matters concerning the girl. They determine that Juliet is almost fourteen, old enough to marry by the custom of the day, and Lady Capulet asks her daughter if she would like to marry Paris. Before Juliet can answer, the nurse and Lady Capulet burst out in praise of Paris's handsomeness. Lady Capulet informs Juliet that she will see Paris at the party tonight and lets her know that even if she is not impressed by his looks, she should be impressed by his status, which she would share if she were to become his wife. Juliet obediently promises to look favorably upon Paris, but only as favorably as her parents will allow.

Act I, scene 4 takes place outside Capulet's house, as Romeo, Benvolio, and a number of friends and fellow Montagues gather before entering the party. In order to protect their identities, the members of Romeo's party are going to the ball as masked dancers, and they pause to discuss the details of their performance. Romeo insists on being a torchbearer, claiming that he is too lovesick to dance. One of Romeo's friends, Mercutio (who is also related to Prince Escalus), teases Romeo unmercifully for not dancing. Romeo states that he had an ominous dream, and Mercutio launches on a long and witty diatribe against taking dreams seriously, claiming that they are simply the mischief of Queen Mab, the fairy midwife. When Romeo accuses Mercutio of talking nonsense, Mercutio counters that dreams are nonsense, but Romeo remains apprehensive.

Act I, scene 5 moves to inside the Capulets' house, where the servants are putting the finishing touches on the dance hall. The Capulets and their guests enter and the masked dancers begin to dance with the ladies as Juliet's father and another elderly Capulet reminisce about their long-gone dancing days. Romeo, holding a torch, spies Juliet and is immediately smitten, asking a servant to identify her (he cannot) and declaiming on her beauty.

Juliet's feisty cousin Tybalt recognizes Romeo's voice and promptly sends for his sword, claiming that he will kill him where he stands. Fortunately for Romeo, old Capulet stops Tybalt, claiming that he does not want a fight at his party and pointing out that Romeo is behaving himself appropriately. Tybalt, however, is still eager to fight and is only deterred by the threat of losing Capulet's favor; he leaves the party, promising revenge. In the meantime, Romeo accosts Juliet, takes her hand, declares his affection, and kisses her twice before her nurse intervenes. Romeo learns from the nurse Juliet's identity; later, after the party breaks up, Juliet learns Romeo's from the same source. Both are distraught by the knowledge, for they have irretrievably fallen in love.

Act II begins with another sonnet from the chorus, who reassures the audience that Romeo's old love is gone and that he and Juliet now love each other. The chorus points out that although the couple has little opportunity to interact, their "passion lends them power, time means, to meet." Their meeting forms the subject of the act, as (**Act II, scene 1**) Romeo hides in the Capulets' garden while his friends, Benvolio and Mercutio, try to find him to take him home. Mercutio mocks Romeo's passion, ridiculing it as vulgar lust. After the two friends finally give up and leave, Romeo bitterly remarks that Mercutio "jests at scars" because he "never felt a wound."

Romeo's comment begins the famous balcony scene (**II.2**). Juliet appears at her window in the house by the garden, and Romeo is astonished yet again by her beauty. "But soft," he exclaims, "what light through yonder window breaks? / It is the east, and Juliet is the sun." Romeo continues to compare Juliet favorably to a host of heavenly beings but hopes that she will steer clear of the moon, which is associated with Diana, the

Roman goddess of the moon and also the patron of virgins. She appears as if she is going to speak; Romeo thinks for a moment of revealing himself but hesitates to disturb her. He watches her lean her cheek against her hand, and then she breaks out with an "Ay me!" which excites the hidden Romeo still more.

Unbeknownst to Romeo, Juliet is equally distraught and lovestruck, and she has evidently gone to the balcony to be alone with her feelings. Thinking herself alone, she begins to bewail her fate in loving a man of a rival family, exclaiming:

> O Romeo, Romeo, wherefore art thou Romeo?
> Deny thy father and refuse thy name;
> Or, if thou wilt not, be but sworn my love,
> And I'll no longer be a Capulet.

Romeo wonders whether to reveal himself but chooses to hear more. Juliet continues to hope aloud that Romeo would forget his familial association and be her love:

> What's in a name? That which we call a rose
> By any other word would smell as sweet;
> So Romeo would, were he not Romeo call'd,
> Retain that dear perfection which he owes
> Without that title. Romeo doff thy name,
> And for thy name, which is no part of thee,
> Take all myself.

Romeo, who can no longer contain himself, emerges from hiding, exclaiming, "Call me but love, and I'll be new baptiz'd." Although Romeo refuses to identify himself by his hated name, Juliet quickly recognizes his voice.

The two converse, and Juliet immediately demonstrates a certain practical streak—her first concerns are to know how Romeo got into her garden and to warn him that if her kinsmen find him he will be killed. Romeo restores the romantic tone, however, exclaiming that he would willingly die for her and that love showed him the way to her window. His professions of love fluster Juliet, who declares that she loves him as well and hopes that he does not find her "too quickly won" or "think [her] behavior light." Romeo attempts to vow his love, but Juliet worries that his promises will be false. She does swear her love, however, and when her nurse calls her away from the window, she tells Romeo to stay. She quickly reappears and tells Romeo that if his "bent of love be honorable," he should arrange for them to be married the next day and send a message telling her where and when to meet him for the wedding. Her nurse calls her away again, and Romeo starts to leave. But Juliet reappears one last time, and the two of them exchange some genuine expressions of affection before she exits again.

In **Act II, scene 3** dawn is breaking on the living quarters of Friar Lawrence (spelled in some texts as Laurence), a Franciscan monk. The friar is preparing to gather healing herbs and reveals a wealth of knowledge of the medicinal properties of plants—knowledge that will figure prominently later on. Romeo enters, and the friar, noting that he has not slept the night before, exclaims that he hopes Romeo was not engaging in illicit activities with Rosaline. Romeo explains that he has forgotten all about Rosaline; he is now in love with Juliet and wants the friar to marry them. The friar echoes the question that is perhaps foremost in the audience's mind: hasn't Romeo been awfully quick to discard Rosaline? At the same time, the friar somewhat unwittingly reinforces the idea that Romeo and Juliet's love is good and special by pointing out that everyone knew Romeo did not really love Rosaline and that marrying the couple will help mend the feud between the Montagues and the Capulets.

The difference between Romeo's love for Juliet and what the friar termed his "doting" on Rosaline is emphasized in the next scene (**II.4**) when Romeo, having left the friar, runs into Benvolio and Mercutio, who are discussing the challenge to a duel that Tybalt sent to the Montague house for Romeo that morning. When they meet up with Romeo, he is far from his former self-dramatizing, melancholy self and instead jests heartily with Mercutio. Juliet's nurse enters with her servant Peter and asks to speak to Romeo alone (which results in an endless amount of snide commentary from Mercutio and Benvolio).

Romeo tells her where and when he and Juliet are to marry, and in the next scene (**II.5**) the nurse returns home, where Juliet anxiously awaits the news. After some teasing and withholding of information (foreshadowing the later unreliable messenger of Friar Lawrence's), the nurse relates the message. The final scene of the act (**II.6**) has Romeo and Friar Lawrence waiting for Juliet in the friar's quarters. The scene is not entirely happy, however; the friar ominously informs the impassioned Romeo, "These violent delights have violent ends, / And in their triumph die, like fire and powder, / Which as they kiss consume." Juliet appears, the two exchange pleasantries, and the friar leads them off to be married.

Act III begins with Benvolio and Mercutio walking the streets of Verona. Mercutio is obviously spoiling for a fight, and when Tybalt appears and begins to ask after Romeo, Mercutio makes it clear that he would like nothing better than to duel. The fight is momentarily delayed, however, when Romeo appears on the scene. Tybalt insults him, but Romeo (aware, as Tybalt is not, that they are now related through marriage) ignores the insult and declares his love for Tybalt. Mercutio, inflamed by what he sees as Romeo's craven submissiveness, draws his sword and challenges Tybalt over Romeo's objections. The two fight; when Romeo tries to break up the duel, Tybalt reaches under Romeo's arm with his sword and stabs Mercutio, then flees the scene.

The wound proves fatal, and Mercutio, lying wounded on the streets of Verona, wishes "A plague a' both your houses!" before Benvolio takes him indoors. Benvolio returns shortly with news of Mercutio's death, just as Tybalt reappears. The grief-stricken Romeo challenges Tybalt, they fight, and Tybalt is slain. By this point the citizens of Verona have been alarmed, and Benvolio points out that if Romeo is accosted by the authorities, he will surely be put to death. Romeo flees the scene, crying "O, I am fortune's fool!"

The authorities enter, looking for the murderer of Mercutio. When Benvolio points out the slain Tybalt to them, he is taken into custody. Prince Escalus and the heads of the Montague and Capulet households appear, and Benvolio recounts the bloody events. Lady Capulet challenges his account, however, claiming that since he is a Montague, his word cannot be trusted. The prince decides to make an example of Romeo and exiles him from Verona on penalty of death.

Act III, scene 2 opens on the blissfully ignorant Juliet, who is breathlessly awaiting the coming of night, when Romeo is to sneak into her room by means of a rope ladder and they are to consummate their marriage. Her nurse, rendered almost speechless with grief, appears with the ladder; in her incoherence she garbles her message and causes Juliet to think that Romeo has been killed. Eventually she makes it clear that Romeo killed Tybalt and has been banished. Juliet is obviously none too happy at either piece of news, but she realizes that she would rather Romeo killed Tybalt than vice versa. The news of his banishment, however, leaves her distraught, and she proposes to hang herself with the rope ladder. The nurse stops her by saying that she knows where he is hiding and will bring him to Juliet that night.

Act III, scene 3 shows Romeo hiding out in Friar Lawrence's quarters. The friar enters and informs Romeo that he has been banished. Like Juliet, Romeo becomes distraught and suicidal at the thought of being separated from his love, and he refuses to hide himself when someone knocks at the door. Fortunately, it is Juliet's nurse, who draws the obvious parallel between the two lovers' miseries. This fails to calm Romeo, however. Upon hearing that he has caused Juliet pain, he attempts to stab himself, but the nurse snatches the dagger away. The friar castigates Romeo for the suicide attempt, telling him that he is being self-indulgent and actually unloving to Juliet, who would certainly follow his example if he killed himself. This perceptive (if somewhat ominous) criticism is followed by the practical advice that Romeo see Juliet that night, then sneak out of Verona and stay in nearby Mantua until the prince can be convinced to forgive him. The nurse praises this sage advice and, after giving Romeo a ring of Juliet's, leaves to give Juliet the news.

The blunt passion of Romeo contrasts strongly with the insensitivity of old Capulet, who appears at home in **Act III, scene 4** with his wife and County Paris. Capulet explains Juliet's absence by pointing out that her cousin was murdered that day, then after claiming that he loved Tybalt, he dismisses his slain kinsman with a callous "Well, we were born to die." Although he has yet to hear his daughter's opinion of Paris, he agrees to marry her to him that coming Wednesday. Upon hearing that it is now Monday night, he exclaims:

> Monday! ha, ha! Well, We'n'sday is too soon,
> A' Thursday let it be—a' Thursday, tell her,
> She shall be married to this noble earl.

As dawn rises the next day (**III.5**), Romeo and Juliet stand at Juliet's balcony, savoring the last minutes of a night of conjugal bliss. Romeo must flee, however, when the nurse brings news that Lady Capulet is coming. The lady and Juliet discuss Tybalt's death and his killer, and Juliet begins what is to become a habit of clever dissembling, hoping aloud that no one aside from herself is given the opportunity to avenge Tybalt's death (she knows, as her mother does not, that this would guarantee Romeo's safety). Her mother tells her to be happy, for she is to marry Paris. Juliet replies that she would rather marry Romeo, a statement Lady Capulet interprets as meaning that Juliet is absolutely uninterested in Paris.

At this point, Capulet enters, and upon hearing of Juliet's refusal, he lashes out at his daughter, claiming that he will drag her bodily to the church if he must. When his wife and Juliet's nurse object to his abusive language, he rails against them as well, finally telling Juliet that he will throw her out on the street to starve if she does not marry Paris. He storms off, his wife follows, and the devastated Juliet turns to the nurse for advice. The nurse's counsel, however, appalls her; she suggests that Juliet marry Paris because he is wealthier and more powerful than Romeo—advice that if followed would make Juliet a bigamist (since her first marriage was consummated and her first husband is living). Hiding her feelings, Juliet tells the nurse that she is comforted and must go to Friar Lawrence to make confession. The nurse goes to tell the parents where Juliet is going, and the young lady swears never to trust her nurse again and determines to stop the wedding either by getting help from the friar or by killing herself.

Act IV begins with Friar Lawrence in his quarters discussing the planned wedding with County Paris. Not surprisingly, the friar attempts to discover if Paris has asked Juliet her opinion of the match. Paris, of course, has not, but he wishes to hold the wedding soon in any case, since it seems that Juliet is mourning Tybalt excessively and the wedding might cheer her up. Juliet enters and is not only unresponsive to Paris's solicitude but implies that the count thinks he owns her. He leaves her with the friar to make her confession, and she tells the friar that he must help her or she will commit suicide.

The friar comes up with a dangerous plot: he has a potion that, when swallowed, makes a person fall into a deathlike coma for a period of forty-two hours. Juliet is to return home and claim that she will accept the marriage, then take the potion that night. The next day when her family finds her, they will believe her dead and inter her in the Capulet tomb. The friar will send a messenger to Romeo in Mantua, who will go to the Capulet tomb and break it open just before she revives. The couple will then be free to live together in Mantua. The plot has its hazards, but Juliet is sure of her courage and readily approves.

Act IV, scene 2 takes place the next day in the Capulet household, where preparations are underway for the upcoming nuptials. Juliet returns from her visit with the friar and tells her parents that Lawrence has chastised her for her disobedience and told her to beg their forgiveness. They are quite pleased at the change of heart, which leads to an intriguing gender switch as Juliet's father offers to "play the huswife" during the wedding preparations. Finally (**IV.3**), Juliet is left alone in her room with the vial of Friar Lawrence's potion. She has some moments of fear: What if the friar gave her poison to conceal his role in this affair? What if she comes out of her coma early and has to lie with Tybalt's festering body in the Capulet tomb? She has a quick vision of Tybalt's ghost, but then she recollects her beloved Romeo, drinks the potion, and collapses upon the bed.

The morning comes (**IV.4**) as the Capulets and the nurse prepare for the wedding. The nurse goes into Juliet's room to wake her and discovers her seeming corpse (**IV.5**). The resulting scene, in which the nurse, Paris, and the Capulets mourn Juliet's death, is almost comic. The phrases the mourners use are like a parody of grief and, at the least, seem to indicate a lack of real feeling for Juliet even at her death. For example, the nurse cries, "She's dead, deceas'd, she's dead, alack the day!" and Lady Capulet replies, "Alack the day, she's dead, she's dead, she's dead!" Paris claims that Juliet has been "Beguil'd, divorced, wronged, spited, slain!" and old Capulet chimes in with "Despis'd, distressed, hated, martyr'd, kill'd!" Much as he earlier chastised Romeo, Friar Lawrence (who arrives to perform the marriage) stops the hysterical mourners with a blunt "Peace ho, for shame!" and berates the hypocritical Capulets:

> The most you sought was her promotion
> For 'twas your heaven she should be advanc'd.
> And weep ye now, seeing she is advanc'd
> Above the clouds, and high as heaven itself?

The friar also takes the opportunity to further his own agenda by suggesting that they place her in the tomb as soon as possible. The wedding party, now a funeral party, departs for the graveyard, leaving the servants and musicians behind to make jokes and connive to get free food.

Act V of the play opens in Mantua, where Romeo is pondering another dream, one where Juliet found him dead and brought him back to life with a kiss. His good mood is destroyed, however, when his servant Balthasar comes in having just arrived from Verona. Juliet is dead, Balthasar tells Romeo; he saw her corpse being placed in the Capulet tomb. Romeo, disbelieving, plans to ride to Verona that night. He then asks Balthasar if there is any news from the friar and, hearing there is none, dismisses the man. Once Balthasar is gone, Romeo reveals his true intentions—he will kill himself with poison at Juliet's tomb. He has noticed a rundown apothecary's shop in the city, and goes there on the assumption that the man's poverty will prompt him to sell poison, an illegal act in Mantua. His hunch proves correct; the apothecary seems a good man but is desperate for money, which Romeo gives him with the caveat that it is "worse poison to men's souls, / Doing more murther in this loathsome world, / Than these poor compounds that thou mayest not sell."

In **Act V, scene 2**, Friar Lawrence runs into Friar John, a fellow Franciscan who was supposed to bring the message of Juliet's ruse to Romeo. John has been trapped in a house afflicted with some sort of plague and was not able to go to Mantua or even send a message. Lawrence, assuming that Romeo is simply ignorant of the whole affair, arranges to send him another message and prepares to break into the Capulet tomb and retrieve the revived Juliet himself, then hide her in his quarters until Romeo comes.

Lawrence is not the only one interested in the Capulet tomb; Paris has decided to strew Juliet's grave with flowers and perfume every night in token of his affection. Night finds him making these rites in the graveyard while his page keeps watch and alerts him to the coming of two men (**V.3**). Paris conceals himself only to see Romeo and Balthasar come to the tomb, armed with equipment to break in. Romeo gives Balthasar a letter to give to his father and tells him in no uncertain terms to leave. Balthasar is suspicious of Romeo's intentions, however, and decides to hide himself nearby. Romeo begins breaking into the tomb, but Paris, recognizing him and assuming he is in the graveyard to defile the Capulet bodies, steps out and challenges him. They fight, frightening off Paris's page, who goes to call the watch.

Romeo fatally wounds his attacker (whose identity he does not know), and the count makes a dying request to be placed in the tomb with Juliet. Romeo realizes that he has killed Paris, Mercutio's kinsman, and vaguely recalls hearing that Paris was to marry Juliet. Although Romeo is not sure that his memory is correct, he honors his rival's last request, bringing him into the tomb. There he sees Juliet's body and, with unintended irony, he remarks on her beauty, which he thinks has been amazingly well-preserved in death. He also notes Tybalt's corpse and hopes that by killing himself he will somehow make amends for that murder. He swears his love for Juliet, embraces her body, and swallows the poison, which quickly kills him.

Immediately after Romeo's death, Friar Lawrence enters the graveyard and happens upon Balthasar, who tells him that

Romeo is in the Capulet tomb. In the entrance to the tomb, the friar sees the blood and weapons from Romeo and Paris's fight; his worries are justified as he goes into the tomb and sees the corpses of the two men. Soon after he enters, Juliet revives, asking after Romeo. The friar, hearing the watch come, quickly tells her that Romeo and Paris are dead and tries to convince her to flee the scene with him. But Juliet stays and, as in Romeo's dream, kisses his corpse, which is still warm. He does not revive, however; instead Juliet hears the arrival of the watch and decides to kill herself with his dagger before they can find and stop her. She stabs herself and dies on Romeo's corpse.

The page and the watch arrive and discover the three bodies. They send messengers to the Montagues, Capulets, and Prince Escalus and scour the area for witnesses, picking up Balthasar and Friar Lawrence. The prince and the Capulets arrive first, followed by old Montague, who reveals that Lady Montague has died of grief because of Romeo's exile. The friar tells the assembled party about Romeo and Juliet's secret marriage and subsequent suicide; the letter Romeo gave Balthasar to give to old Montague confirms the friar's tale. The prince decides that this tragedy is divine retribution for the Capulet-Montague feud, telling the patriarchs:

> See what a scourge is laid upon your hate,
> That heaven finds means to kill your joys with love.
> And I for winking at your discords too
> Have lost a brace of kinsmen. All are punish'd.

Old Capulet and Montague swear to end their hostilities, and each offers to raise a gold statue of the other's child. The prince ends the play on an appropriately mournful note:

> A glooming peace this morning with it brings,
> The sun, for sorrow, will not show his head.
> Go hence to have more talk of these sad things;
> Some shall be pardon'd, and some punished:
> For never was a story of more woe
> Than this of Juliet and her Romeo. ❖

—Mary B. Sisson

List of Characters

Romeo is the son of the house of Montague, a wealthy Verona family, and is a young, romantic man. He seems relatively uninvolved in the feud between his family and the Capulets, another wealthy family in the city, and in the course of the play he falls deeply in love with the Capulets' daughter, Juliet. They secretly marry, but events cause Romeo to kill her cousin, Tybalt, and be exiled from the city. Upon hearing a false account of Juliet's death, Romeo goes to her tomb and poisons himself.

Juliet is the daughter of the house of Capulet, which is engaged in a bloody feud with Romeo's family, the Montagues. Juliet, who at the beginning of the play seems merely a young, naive, and obedient daughter, falls in love with Romeo and marries him. She reveals herself to be tough-minded and courageous when her secret marriage with Romeo is threatened by her father's decision to marry her to Paris. She eventually participates in an elaborate plan to avoid the second marriage by feigning her own death. The plan backfires when Romeo, believing her dead, commits suicide; upon discovering his corpse, Juliet fatally stabs herself.

Friar Lawrence, a Franciscan monk, performs the secret wedding of Romeo and Juliet and devises the scheme by which Juliet attempts to avoid marrying Paris. The friar is a learned man and offers generally wise advice to a number of other characters; however, the scheme he proposes to Juliet eventually leads to the deaths of her, Paris, and Romeo.

Juliet's Nurse is a dedicated and loyal if somewhat empty-headed ally of Juliet and plays an important role in getting Romeo and Juliet secretly married. Her lack of moral center causes Juliet to discard her as a confidante, however; she suggests that Juliet marry Paris despite her existing marriage to Romeo because Paris is richer.

Paris, kin to Prince Escalus and Mercutio, is a wealthy nobleman who wishes to marry Juliet. Although he seems a decent man, he is blind to the fact that Juliet does not care for him and does not want to marry him. He is eventually killed by Romeo, whom he attacks when he thinks Romeo is breaking into the Capulet tomb to defile the bodies.

Old Capulet is the head of the Capulet household and Juliet's father. He condones the feud with the Montagues but displays a certain restraint when he prevents Tybalt from attacking Romeo at a party. His character becomes less sympathetic, however, when he attempts to force Juliet to marry the wealthy and powerful Paris. After Romeo and Juliet's suicides, he swears friendship with old Montague.

Tybalt, the nephew of Juliet's mother, is an extremely violent and pugnacious young man who kills Romeo's friend Mercutio and is in turn killed by Romeo, causing Romeo to be exiled from Verona.

Mercutio is a witty and punning young nobleman and kin to both Paris and Prince Escalus. Although he is not a Montague, he takes their side in the feud, an attitude that causes him to challenge Tybalt, who kills him.

Benvolio, the nephew of old Montague, is a calm and reasonable character who attempts to keep the peace in Verona in the face of an escalating feud.

Prince Escalus is the ruler of Verona who exiles Romeo in an attempt to end the Capulet-Montague feud, which he feels is a disturbance and a menace to the citizens of his city.

Lady Capulet, Juliet's mother and Tybalt's aunt, encourages Juliet to marry Paris but objects to her husband's abusive behavior when her daughter refuses.

Old Montague is head of the Montague household and Romeo's father. He obviously cares for his son but encourages the feud that results in his banishment, which causes Lady Montague to die from grief and ultimately leads to Romeo's suicide. ❖

Critical Views

[Samuel Johnson (1709–1784) was perhaps the greatest British critic and man of letters in the eighteenth century. Among his major works are the novel *Rasselas* (1759) and *Lives of the English Poets* (1779–81). In this extract, taken from the notes to his edition of Shakespeare (1765), Johnson praises the various characters in *Romeo and Juliet,* especially Mercutio and the Nurse.]

This play is one of the most pleasing of our author's performances. The scenes are busy and various, the incidents numerous and important, the catastrophe irresistibly affecting, and the process of the action carried on with such probability, at least with such congruity to popular opinions, as tragedy requires.

Here is one of the few attempts of Shakespeare to exhibit the conversation of gentlemen, to represent the airy sprightliness of juvenile elegance. Mr. Dryden mentions a tradition, which might easily reach his time, of a declaration made by Shakespeare, that "he was obliged to kill Mercutio in the third act, lest he should have been killed by him." Yet he thinks him "no such formidable person, but that he might have lived through the play, and died in his bed," without danger to a poet. Dryden well knew, had he been in quest of truth, that, in a pointed sentence, more regard is commonly had to the words than the thought, and that it is very seldom to be rigorously understood. Mercutio's wit, gaiety and courage, will always procure him friends that wish him a longer life; but his death is not precipitated, he has lived out the time allotted him in the construction of the play; nor do I doubt the ability of Shakespeare to have continued his existence, though some of his sallies are perhaps out of the reach of Dryden; whose genius was not very fertile of merriment, nor ductile to humour, but acute, argumentative, comprehensive, and sublime.

The Nurse is one of the characters in which the authour delighted: he has, with great subtilty of distinction, drawn her at once loquacious and secret, obsequious and insolent, trusty and dishonest.

His comick scenes are happily wrought, but his pathetick strains are always polluted with some unexpected depravations. His persons, however distressed, "have a conceit left them in their misery, a miserable conceit" ⟨John Dryden⟩.

—Samuel Johnson, *The Plays of William Shakespeare* (London: J. & R. Tonson, 1765), Vol. 8, p. 124

❖

AUGUST WILHELM VON SCHLEGEL ON THE MERITS OF *ROMEO AND JULIET*

[August Wilhelm von Schlegel (1767–1845), German Romanticist and literary critic, translated the works of Shakespeare into German. He is the author of a series of lectures, *Über dramatische Kunst und Literatur* (1809–11), in which Shakespeare is extensively discussed. In this extract from that work, Schlegel praises Shakespeare's dramatic structure and richness of detail, but argues that the true merit of *Romeo and Juliet* comes from the beauty of the author's sentiments on the nature of love.]

Romeo and Juliet, and *Othello,* differ from most of the pieces which we have hitherto examined, neither in the ingredients of the composition, nor in the manner of treating them: it is merely the direction of the whole that gives them the stamp of Tragedy. *Romeo and Juliet* is a picture of love and its pitiable fate, in a world whose atmosphere is too sharp for this the tenderest blossom of human life. Two beings created for each other feel mutual love at the first glance; every consideration disappears before the irresistible impulse to live in one another; under circumstances hostile in the highest degree to their union, they unite themselves by a secret marriage, relying simply on the protection of an invisible power. Untoward incidents following in rapid succession, their heroic constancy is within a few days put to the proof, till, forcibly separated from each other, by a voluntary death they are united in the grave to meet again in another world. All this is to be found in the beautiful story which Shakspeare has not invented, and which, however simply told, will always excite a gender sympathy: but it was reserved for Shakspeare to join in one ideal picture purity of heart with warmth of imagination; sweetness and dignity of manners with passionate intensity of feeling. Under his handling, It has become a glorious song of praise on that inexpressible feeling which ennobles the soul and gives to it its highest sublimity, and which elevates even the senses into soul, while at the same time it is a melancholy elegy on its inherent and imparted frailty; it is at once the apotheosis and the obsequies of love. It appears here a heavenly spark, that, as it descends to the earth, is converted into the lightning flash, which almost in the same moment sets on fire and consumes the mortal being on whom it lights. All that is most intoxicating in the odour of a southern spring,—all that is languishing in the song of the nightingale, or voluptuous in the first opening of the rose, all alike breathe forth from this poem. But even more rapidly than the earliest blossoms of youth and beauty decay, does it from the first timidly-bold declaration and modest return of love hurry on to the most unlimited passion, to an irrevocable union; and then hastens, amidst alternating storms of rapture and despair, to the fate of the two lovers, who yet appear enviable in their hard lot, for their love survives them, and by their death they have obtained an endless triumph over every separating power. The sweetest and the bitterest love and hatred, festive rejoicings and dark forebodings, tender embraces and sepulchral horrors, the fulness of life and self-annihilation, are here all brought close to each other; and yet these contrasts are so blended into a unity of impression, that the echo which the whole leaves behind in the mind resembles a single but endless sigh.

The excellent dramatic arrangement, the significance of every character in its place, the judicious selection of all the circumstances, even the most minute, have already been dwelt upon in detail. I shall only request attention to a trait which may serve for an example of the distance to which Shakspeare goes back to lay the preparatory foundation. The most striking and perhaps incredible circumstance in the whole story is the liquor given by the Monk to Julia, by which she for a number of hours not merely sleeps, but fully resembles a corpse, without however receiving the least injury. How does the poet dispose us to believe that Father Lorenzo possesses such a secret?—At his first appearance he exhibits him in a garden, where he is collecting herbs and descanting on their wonderful virtues. The discourse of the pious old man is full of deep meaning: he sees everywhere in nature emblems of the moral world; the same wisdom with which he looks through her has also made him master of the human heart. In this manner a circumstance of an ungrateful appearance, has become the source of a great beauty.

> —August Wilhelm von Schlegel, *A Course of Lectures on Dramatic Art and Literature* (1809–11), tr. John Black (London: Henry G. Bohn, 1846), pp. 400–401

❧

WILLIAM HAZLITT ON THE REALISM OF *ROMEO AND JULIET*

[William Hazlitt (1778–1830), one of the greatest critics of the nineteenth century, wrote such works as *Lectures on the English Poets* (1818), *Lectures on the English Comic Writers* (1819), and a poignant book on his love for a prostitute, *Liber Amoris* (1823). In this extract from his study of Shakespeare's characters, Hazlitt refutes those who maintain that *Romeo and Juliet* is unrealistic in its portrayal of the love between two young people.]

Romeo and Juliet is the only tragedy which Shakespear has written entirely on a love-story. It is supposed to have been his first play, and it deserves to stand in that proud rank. There is the buoyant spirit of youth in every line, in the rapturous intoxication of hope, and in the bitterness of despair. It has been said of *Romeo and Juliet* by a great critic, that 'whatever is most intoxicating in the odour of a southern spring, languishing in the song of the nightingale, or voluptuous in the first opening of the rose, is to be found in this poem.' The description is true; and yet it does not answer to our idea of the play. For if it has the sweetness of the rose, it has its freshness too; if it has the languor of the nightingale's song, it has also its giddy transport; if it has the softness of a southern spring, it is as glowing and as bright. There is nothing of a sickly and sentimental cast. Romeo and Juliet are in love, but they are not love-sick. Every thing speaks the very soul of pleasure, the high and healthy pulse of the passions: the heart beats, the blood circulates and mantles throughout. Their courtship is not an insipid interchange of sentiments lip-deep, learnt at second-hand from poems and plays,—made up of beauties of the most shadowy kind, of 'fancies wan that hang the pensive head,' of evanescent smiles, and sighs that breathe not, of delicacy that shrinks from the touch, and feebleness that scarce supports itself, an elaborate vacuity of thought, and an artificial dearth of sense, spirit, truth, and nature! It is the reverse of all this. It is Shakespear all over, and Shakespear when he was young.

We have heard it objected to *Romeo and Juliet,* that it is founded on an idle passion between a boy and a girl, who have scarcely seen and can have but little sympathy or rational esteem for one another, who have had no experience of the good or ills of life, and whose raptures or despair must be therefore equally groundless and fantastical. Whoever objects to the youth of the parties in this play as 'too unripe and crude' to pluck the sweets of love, and wishes to see a first-love carried on into a good old age, and the passions taken at the rebound, when their force is spent, may find all this done in the *Stranger* and in other German plays, where they do things by contraries, and transpose nature to inspire sentiment and create philosophy. Shakespear proceeded in a more straitforward, and, we think, effectual way. He did not endeavour to extract beauty from wrinkles, or the wild throb of passion from the last expiring sigh of indifference. He did not 'gather grapes of thorns nor figs of thistles.' It was not his way. But he has given a picture of human life, such as it is in the order of nature. He has founded the passion of the two lovers not on the pleasures they had experienced, but on all the pleasures they had *not* experienced. All that was to come of life was theirs. At that untried source of promised happiness they slaked their thirst, and the first eager draught made them drunk with love and joy. They were in full possession of their senses and their affections. Their hopes were of air, their desires of fire. Youth is the season of love, because the heart is then first melted in tenderness from the touch of novelty, and kindled to rapture, for it knows no end of its enjoyments or its wishes. Desire has no limit but itself. Passion, the love and expectation of pleasure, is infinite, extravagant, inexhaustible, till experience comes to check and kill it. Juliet exclaims on her first interview with Romeo—

> My bounty is as boundless as the sea,
> My love as deep.

And why should it not? What was to hinder the thrilling tide of pleasure, which had just gushed from her heart, from flowing on without stint or measure, but experience which she was yet without? What was to abate the transport of the first sweet sense of pleasure, which her heart and her senses had just tasted, but indifference which she was yet a stranger to? What was there to check the ardour of hope, of faith, of constancy, just rising in her breast, but disappointment which she had not yet felt! As are the desires and the hopes of youthful passion, such is the keenness of its disappointments, and their baleful effect. Such is the transition in this play from the highest bliss to the lowest despair, from the nuptial couch to an untimely grave. The only evil that even in apprehension befalls the two lovers is the loss of the greatest possible felicity; yet this loss is fatal to both, for they had rather part with life than bear the thought of surviving all that had made life dear to them. In all this, Shakespear has but followed nature, which existed in his time, as well as now. The modern philosophy, which reduces the whole theory of the mind to habitual impressions, and leaves the natural impulses of passion and imagination out of the account, had not then been discovered; or if it had, would have been little calculated for the uses of poetry.

—William Hazlitt, *Characters of Shakespear's Plays* (1817), *The Collected Works of William Hazlitt,* ed. A. R. Waller and Arnold Glover (London: J. M. Dent, 1902), Vol. 1, pp. 248–50

❖

CHARLES KNIGHT ON THE HISTORICAL BACKGROUND OF
ROMEO AND JULIET

[Charles Knight (1791–1873), a prolific literary critic
and Shakespeare scholar, is the author of *William
Shakspere: A Biography* (1843) and *Half-Hours with
the Best Authors* (1848). He also produced an edition
of Shakespeare's works. In this extract from his *Studies
of Shakspere* (1849), Knight comments on the historical
background of *Romeo and Juliet*.]

The slight foundation of historical truth which can be established in the legend of *Romeo and Juliet*—that of the "civil
broils" of the two rival houses of Verona—would place the
period of the action about the time of Dante. But this one circumstance ought not, as it appears to us, very strictly to limit
this period. The legend is so obscure, that we may be justified
in carrying its date forward or backward, to the extent even of
a century, if anything may be gained by such a freedom. In this
case, we may venture to associate the story with the period
which followed the times of Petrarch and Boccaccio—verging
towards the close of the fourteenth century—a period full of
rich associations. Then, the literary treasures of the ancient
world had been rescued out of the dust and darkness of
ages,—the language of Italy had been formed, in great part, by
the marvellous *Visions* of her greatest poet; painting had been
revived by Giotto and Cimabue; architecture had put on a character of beauty and majesty, and the first necessities of shelter
and defence had been associated with the higher demands of
comfort and taste; sculpture had displayed itself in many beautiful productions, both in marble and bronze; and music had
been cultivated as a science. All these were the growth of the
freedom which prevailed in the Italian republics, and of the
wealth which had been acquired by commercial enterprise,
under the impulses of freedom. To date the period of the action
of *Romeo and Juliet* before this revival of learning and the arts,
would be to make its accessories out of harmony with the
exceeding beauty of Shakspere's drama. Even if a slight portion
of historical accuracy be sacrificed, his poetry must be
surrounded with an appropriate atmosphere of grace and
richness.

"Of the truth of Juliet's story, they (the Veronese) seem tenacious to a degree,—insisting on the fact, giving a date (1303), and showing a tomb. It is a plain, open, and partly decayed sarcophagus, with withered leaves in it, in a wild and desolate conventual garden, once a cemetery, now ruined to the very graves. The situation struck me as very appropriate to the legend, being blighted as their love." Byron thus described the tomb of Juliet to his friend ⟨Thomas⟩ Moore, as he saw it at the close of autumn, when withered leaves had dropped into the decayed sarcophagus, and the vines that are trailed above it had been stripped of their fruit. His letter to Moore, in which this passage occurs, is dated the 7th November. But this wild and desolate garden only struck Byron as appropriate to the *legend*—to that simple tale of fierce hatreds and fatal loves which tradition has still preserved, amongst those who may never have read Luigi da Porto or Bandello, and who, perhaps, never heard the name of Shakspere. To the legend only is the blighted place appropriate. For who that has ever been thoroughly imbued with the story of Juliet, as told by Shakspere,—who that has heard his "glorious song of praise on that inexpressible feeling which ennobles the soul and gives to it its highest sublimity, and which elevates even the senses themselves into soul,"—who that, in our great poet's matchless delineation of Juliet's love, has perceived "whatever is most intoxicating in the odour of a southern spring, languishing in the song of the nightingale, or voluptuous on the first opening of the rose,"—who, indeed, that looks upon the tomb of the Juliet of Shakspere, can see only a shapeless ruin amidst wildness and desolation?

> A grave? Oh, no; a lantern, . . .
> For here lies Juliet, and her beauty makes
> This vault a feasting presence full of light.

—Charles Knight, *Studies of Shakspere* (London: Charles Knight, 1849), pp. 218–19

❖

George Bernard Shaw on the Difficulties of Staging Shakespeare

[George Bernard Shaw (1856–1950), the greatest British dramatist of his age, was also a frequent critic. Among his critical works are *The Quintessence of Ibsenism* (1891) and *Dramatic Opinions and Essays* (1906). In this extract, Shaw, who often regarded Shakespeare with a jaundiced eye, asserts that Shakespeare's dialogue in *Romeo and Juliet* is difficult for modern actors to speak because it is based purely upon feeling without thought or substance.]

It should never be forgotten in judging an attempt to play Romeo and Juliet that the parts are made almost impossible, except to actors of positive genius, skilled to the last degree in metrical declamation, by the way in which the poetry, magnificent as it is, is interlarded by the miserable rhetoric and silly logical conceits which were the foible of the Elizabethans. When Juliet comes out on her balcony and, having propounded the question, "What's in a name?" proceeds to argue it out like an amateur attorney in Christmas-card verse of the "rose by any other name" order, no actress can make it appear natural to a century which has discovered the art of giving prolonged and intense dramatic expression to pure feeling alone, without any skeleton of argument or narrative, by means of music. Romeo has lines that tighten the heart or catch you up into the heights, alternately with heartless fustian and silly ingenuities that make you curse Shakespear's stagestruckness and his youthful inability to keep his brains quiet.

—George Bernard Shaw, "*Romeo and Juliet*" (1895), *Shaw on Shakespeare*, ed. Edwin Wilson (New York: E. P. Dutton, 1961), pp. 181–82

❖

FREDERICK S. BOAS ON POLITICAL ELEMENTS IN *ROMEO AND JULIET*

[Frederick S. Boas (1862–1957) wrote extensively on the history of drama. His publications include *An Introduction to Tudor Drama* (1933) and *An Introduction to Stuart Drama* (1946). In this extract from his book on Shakespeare, Boas examines the political rivalry between the Montagues and the Capulets and its tragic consequences for Romeo and Juliet.]

It has been seen that in several of Shakspere's plays there is an enveloping political plot. The peculiarity of *Romeo and Juliet* is that the political plot does not merely form the background to the main action, but is one of its integral elements. The rivalry of the Montagues and the Capulets gives a tragic bias to what would otherwise be a story of youthful love, and it is therefore rightly made the subject of the opening scene. The biting of thumbs by the serving-men, pugnacious within the safe limits of the law, prepares the way for the entrance of Tybalt, the champion of the Capulet claims, the professional duellist with the lore of the fencing school at his finger-tips, who 'fights as you sing prick-song, keeps time, distance, and proportion: rests me his minim rest, one, two, and the third in your bosom.' To such a swashbuckler even the mild Benvolio's presence is a call to arms, and the result is speedily a general fray swollen by partisans of either house, and by citizens who hate both equally, till the entrance of the Prince stops the tumult on pain of death. Thus the rival families are marshalled face to face at the very outset of the action, and the chief of the state, though he is seen for only the briefest interval, launches the edict which is to have fateful consequences hereafter.

From the ranks of the Montague swordsmen there has been one remarkable absentee. The aged head of the house has flourished his blade in defence of the family honour, but Romeo, the son and heir, is nowhere to be seen. His mother's anxious inquiry elicits the news that he has been espied before dawn, stealing alone towards a grove of sycamore, and we further learn that such is his wont, and that at the first streak of light he creeps home to his chamber where he pens himself in artificial night. We are thus warned, before Romeo appears in person, that he is apart from his kinsmen in nature and sympathies. There is a sentimental strain in his character, and at the outset he and Proteus, though they develop so differently, have a certain likeness. His entrance gives the key to his strange humour. He is in love with the lady Rosaline, but his suit is in vain. Hence his passion for solitude, his sighs, and his tears. But neither the love nor the misery, we are persuaded, can be very deep that finds its vent in unmeaning fantastic antithesis, the *reductio ad absurdum* of 'the numbers that Petrarch flowed in.' A heart that is really breaking does not explode in verbal fireworks about 'anything of nothing first created.' This calf-love of Romeo is adopted by Shakspere from Brooke, and it is probably a mistake to invest it with too great significance. That there enters into Romeo's character a vein of weakness, of volatile emotion, cannot be denied, but it is important to notice that whenever Shakspere gives it prominence he is following closely in the wake of Brooke, and that in the scenes due to his own invention the more sterling and genuinely impassioned side of his hero's nature is developed. The retention of the Rosaline episode is very possibly due to the fact that it prepares the way for one of those instances of the irony of fortune which stud the drama. Benvolio bids Romeo attend the feast of the Capulets that he may forget his mistress in the light of other eyes, and Romeo, though he assents, does so with protestations of unswerving fidelity to Rosaline. But even while he is on the way to the palace of the rival house, he is haunted by presentiments that his fate is not in his own hands:

> My mind misgives
> Some consequence, yet hanging in the stars,
> Shall bitterly begin his fearful date
> With this night's revels.

And so it proves: Romeo has but to change eyes with Juliet, and his love in idleness for Rosaline is annihilated, only to give place to a far more absorbing passion. Benvolio's well-meant panacea becomes the root of a direr malady than it was devised to cure.

—Frederick S. Boas, *Shakspere and His Predecessors* (New York: Scribner's, 1896), pp. 201–3

❖

MARK VAN DOREN ON THE LITERARINESS OF *ROMEO AND JULIET*

[Mark Van Doren (1894–1972), the younger brother of Carl Van Doren, was an American critic, poet, and novelist. His *Collected Poems* (1939) won a Pulitzer prize. Among his critical works are *Henry David Thoreau* (1916) and *The Poetry of John Dryden* (1931). In this extract from his book on Shakespeare, Van Doren argues that *Romeo and Juliet* is a youthful play in which there is perhaps an excessive amount of consciously literary artistry.]

When Juliet learns that Romeo has killed Tybalt she cries out that he is a beautiful tyrant, a fiend angelical, a dove-feathered raven, a wolfish lamb, a damned saint, an honorable villain. This echoes Romeo's outcry upon the occasion of Tybalt's first brawl in the streets of Verona: brawling love, loving hate, heavy lightness, serious vanity, chaos of forms, feather of lead, bright smoke, cold fire, sick health, still-waking sleep—Romeo had feasted his tongue upon such opposites, much in the manner of Lucrece when wanton modesty, lifeless life, and cold fire were the only terms that could express her mind's disorder. Of Romeo's lines, says Dr. Johnson, "neither the sense nor the occasion is very evident. He is not yet in love with an enemy, and to love one and hate another is no such uncommon state as can deserve all this toil of antithesis." And of the pathetic strains in *Romeo and Juliet* generally Dr. Johnson adds that they "are always polluted with some unexpected depravations. His persons, however distressed, have a conceit left them in their misery, a miserable conceit."

Romeo and Juliet, in other words, is still a youthful play; its author, no less than its hero and heroine, is furiously literary. He has written at last a tragedy which is crowded with life, and which will become one of the best-known stories in the world; but it is crowded at the same time with clevernesses, it keeps the odor of ink. Images of poison and the grave are common throughout the dialogue, and they fit the fable. The frame of the author's mind is equally fitted, however, by a literary imagery. There is much about words, books, and reading; as indeed there is in *Hamlet,* but with a difference. The servant who delivers Capulet's invitations to the feast cannot distinguish the names on his list, and must have Romeo's help (I, ii). Lady Capulet commands Juliet to

> Read o'er the volume of young Paris' face
> And find delight writ there with beauty's pen; . . .
> This precious book of love, this unbound lover,
> To beautify him, only lacks a cover.   (I, iii, 81–8)

Romeo's first kiss to Juliet, she remarks, is given "by the book" (I, v, 112). Love can suggest to Romeo (II, ii, 157–8) the way of schoolboys with their books. Mercutio with his last breath accuses Tybalt of fighting by "the book of arithmetic" (III, i, 106). Juliet, continuing in her rage against Romeo because he has killed her cousin, demands to know:

> Was ever book containing such vile matter
> So fairly bound?   (II, ii, 83–4)

And words seem to be tangible things. Romeo wishes his name were written down so that he could tear it (II, ii, 57); when the Nurse tells him how Juliet has cried out upon his name it is to him

> As if that name,
> Shot from the deadly level of a gun,
> Did murder her.   (III, iii, 102–4)

And the lovers take eloquent turns (III, ii, iii) at playing variations on "that word 'banished,'" which can "mangle" them and is indeed but "death mis-term'd."

Even the wit of Romeo and his friends—or, as Dr. Johnson puts it, "the airy sprightliness" of their "juvenile elegance"— has a somewhat printed sound. When Romeo, going to the ball, wants to say that the burden of his passion for Rosaline weighs him down and makes him less wanton than his friends he resorts once again to the literary idiom:

> For I am proverb'd with a grandsire phrase.　　　　(I, iv, 37)

Not that the wit of these young gentlemen is poor. It is Shakespeare's best thus far, and it is as brisk as early morning; the playful youths are very knowing and proud, and speak always—until the sudden moment when lightness goes out of the play like a lamp—as if there were no language but that of sunrise and spring wind.

Lightness goes out suddenly with the death of Mercutio. Yet everything is sudden in this play. Its speed is as great as that of *Macbeth,* though it carries no such weight of tragedy. The impatience of the lovers for each other and the brevity of their love are answered everywhere: by Juliet's complaint at the unwieldly slowness with which the Nurse returns from Romeo, by Capulet's testiness as he rushes the preparations for the wedding, by the celerity of the catastrophe once its fuse has been laid.

　　　—Mark Van Doren, *Shakespeare* (New York: Henry Holt, 1939), pp. 65–67

✣

VIRGIL K. WHITAKER ON SHAKESPEARE'S DEVELOPMENT

[Virgil K. Whitaker (b. 1908), a prolific author and literary critic, has written *The Religious Basis of Spenser's Thought* (1950), *Francis Bacon's Intellectual Milieu* (1962), and *The Mirror to Nature: The Technique of Shakespeare's Tragedies* (1965). In this extract, from his study of Shakespeare's learning, Whitaker comments on some of Shakespeare's influences, including Arthur Brooke's *Romeus and Juliet* (1562), and their role in Shakespeare's dramatic development.]

⟨. . .⟩ the play also reveals Shakespeare's increasing knowledge of contemporary poetry and an attempt to interpret his material philosophically. His control of poetry was, however, uncertain, and his fund of ideas was inadequate. These two considerations make *Romeo and Juliet* indicative of the ways in which Shakespeare's learning and thought were developing.

Stylistically the play is noteworthy for its extreme unevenness and for its experiments with various poetic forms. The range from rhetorical bombast to some of Shakespeare's greatest poetry is undoubtedly due in considerable part to the influence of Brooke's *Romeus and Juliet,* which supplied the example and even the material for some of the worst ranting. Granville-Barker notes that the hysterics of Romeo's scene with Friar Lawrence (III, iii) are taken, "at one point all but word for word," from Brooke, and the same might be said of Juliet's preceding scene, except for the wonderful epithalamium with which it opens. Obviously Shakespeare was still depending upon his source for poetic guidance. But Shakespeare quite unassisted by his source must be held guilty of the outrageous lines in which the Nurse, Paris, and Capulet lament Juliet's death, lines which have been identified as a parody of the *Spanish Tragedy.* They actually differ little, if at all, from some of the outright parody that Shakespeare wrote for the "very tragical mirth" of Pyramus and Thisbe, and they, too, show how uncertain his taste must still have been. On the other hand, he has spared us some of Brooke's more maudlin poetry—for example, by restricting Romeo's final scene with Juliet to their farewell, for obvious reasons of propriety as well as of dramatic economy. The episodes of his own invention, which will be listed below, are much better poetically than those derived from the source, and, in general, the really great poetry in the play occurs in them—Mercutio's speeches, the balcony scene, and Juliet's epithalamium. Even in two scenes which as a whole follow Brooke—the meeting of Romeo and Juliet at the party and their deaths in the tomb—the best poetry is not derived from the source.

—Virgil K. Whitaker, *Shakespeare's Use of Learning: An Inquiry into the Growth of his Mind and Art* (San Marino, CA: Huntington Library, 1953), pp. 106–7

❖

M. M. MAHOOD ON SHAKESPEARE'S USE OF PUNS

[M. M. Mahood is the author of *Poetry and Humanism* (1970), *Bit Parts in Shakespeare's Plays* (1992), and *Shakespeare's Wordplay* (1957), from which the following extract is taken. Here, Mahood argues that the many puns and other instances of wordplay in *Romeo and Juliet* are an essential part of the drama, used to vent the characters' emotions and to advance the plot.]

Romeo and Juliet is one of Shakespeare's most punning plays; even a really conservative count yields a hundred and seventy-five quibbles. Critics who find this levity unseemly excuse it by murmuring, with the Bad Quarto Capulet, that "youth's a jolly thing" even in a tragedy. Yet Shakespeare was over thirty, with a good deal of dramatic writing already to his credit, when *Romeo and Juliet* was first performed. He knew what he was about in his wordplay, which is as functional here as in any of his later tragedies. It holds together the play's imagery in a rich pattern and gives an outlet to the tumultuous feelings of the central characters. By its proleptic second and third meanings it serves to sharpen the play's dramatic irony. Above all, it clarifies the conflict of incompatible truths and helps to establish their final equipoise.

Shakespeare's sonnet-prologue offers us a tale of star-crossed lovers and 'The *fearfull passage* of their *death-markt loue*'. *Death-marked* can mean marked out for (or by) death; foredoomed'. If, however, we take *passage* in the sense of a voyage (and this sub-meaning prompts *trafficque* in the twelfth line) as well as a course of events, *death-marked* recalls the 'euer fixed marke' of Sonnet 116 and the sea-mark of Othello's utmost sail and suggests the meaning "With death as their objective." The two meanings of *fearful* increase the line's oscillation; the meaning "frightened" makes the lovers helpless, but they are not necessarily so if the word means 'fearsome' and so suggests that we, the audience, are awe-struck by their undertaking. These ambiguities pose the play's fundamental question at the outset: is its ending frustration or fulfilment? Does Death choose the lovers or do they elect to die? This question emerges from the language of the play itself and thus differs from the conventional, superimposed problem: is *Romeo and Juliet* a tragedy of Character or of Fate? which can be answered only by a neglect or distortion of the play as a dramatic experience. To blame or excuse the lovers' impetuosity and the connivance of others is to return to Arthur Broke's disapproval of unhonest desire, stolen contracts, drunken gossips and auricular confession. Recent critics have, I believe, come nearer to defining the play's experience when they have stressed the *Liebestod* of the ending and suggested that the love of Romeo and Juliet is the tragic passion that seeks its own destruction. Certainly nearly all the elements of the *amour-passion* myth as it has been defined by Denis de Rougemont are present in the play. The love of Romeo and Juliet is immediate, violent and final. In the voyage imagery of the play they abandon themselves to a rudderless course that must end in shipwreck:

> Thou desperate Pilot, now at once run on
> The dashing Rocks, thy seasick weary barke:
> Heeres to my Loue. (V, iii, 117–19)

The obstacle which is a feature of the *amour-passion* legend is partly external, the family feud; but it is partly a sword of the lovers' own tempering since, unlike earlier tellers of the story, Shakespeare leaves us with no explanation of why Romeo did not put Juliet on his horse and make for Mantua. A *leitmotiv* of the play is Death as Juliet's bridegroom; it first appears when Juliet sends to find Romeo's name: "if he be married, My graue is like to be my wedding bed." At the news of Romeo's banishment Juliet cries "And death not Romeo, take my maiden head," and she begs her mother, rather than compel her to marry Paris, to "make the Bridall bed / In that dim Monument where Tibalt lies." The theme grows too persistent to be mere dramatic irony:

> O sonne, the night before thy wedding day
> Hath death laine with thy wife, there she lies,
> Flower as she was, deflowred by him,
> Death is my sonne in law, death is my heire.
> My daughter he hath wedded. (IV, v, 35–9)

Romeo, gazing at the supposedly dead Juliet, could well believe

> that vnsubstantiall death is amorous,
> And that the leane abhorred monster keepes
> Thee here in darke to be his parramour. (V, iii, 103–5)

Most significant of all, there is Juliet's final cry:

> O *happy* dagger
> This is thy sheath, there rust and let me *dye*. (V, iii, 169–70)

where *happy* implies not only "fortunate to me in being ready to my hand" but also 'successful, fortunate in itself' and so suggests a further quibble on *die*. Death has long been Romeo's rival and enjoys Juliet at the last.
> —M. M. Mahood, *"Romeo and Juliet," Shakespeare's Wordplay*
> (London: Methuen, 1957), pp. 56–58

❖

JOHN LAWLOR ON THE ROLE OF *ROMEO AND JULIET* IN SHAKESPEARE'S DEVELOPMENT

[John Lawlor (b. 1918) has lectured at Oxford and many other universities. He is the author of *The Tragic Sense in Shakespeare* (1960), *Chaucer* (1969), and *Piers Plowman: An Essay in Criticism* (1962). In this extract, Lawlor studies the relation that *Romeo and Juliet* occupies in Shakespeare's development as a tragic playwright.]

In *Romeo and Juliet,* the limits within which the human figure can be treated as agent are clear in the activity of mortals—Nurse and Friar, father and mother, friend and clan-enemy—who would bend others to their designs. For this activity serves only to leave those others more clearly the victims of mischance when it comes, without raising problems of character-connection, the relation between what they are and what they must suffer.

The great difference between *Romeo and Juliet* and later tragedies is the exploration of this connection: and Shakespeare's entry upon it is in terms of a purposeful evil, an evil which would seek not merely the downfall but the extinction of all that is other than itself; Aaron is the crude but substantial prototype of Iago. It is therefore true that Shakespeare's tragic development 'does not exactly proceed through *Romeo and Juliet*' ⟨J. C. Maxwell⟩; though the elements common to earlier and later tragic plays should not be overlooked in any simplified account of the 'tragedy of character'. If we seek the line of development from *Romeo and Juliet* we may find it not in the later tragedies but in the antitype of *tragedie,* those last plays of Shakespeare where the scope of accident includes the truth of fortunate accident, so that ancient wrongs are righted and the old make way for newness of life in the young; where fulfilment is achieved in this world and not in a region beyond the stars, even death itself being cancelled and the exile returned to his native land; where all, in fine, is subject to a Time which is not envious or calumniating but, joining with mortal designs, 'Goes upright with his carriage'. Such dramatic work, like *Romeo and Juliet* itself, is not to be dismissed by easy reference to 'the magic of Shakespeare's poetic genius' and 'the intermittent force of his dramatic power' as against any 'grasp of the foundations' of dramatic art (H. B. Charlton). In *Macbeth* a sure grasp of the foundations of tragedy reaffirms that the attempt to bind time is an inherent impossibility: and there all a mature playwright's understanding of his art persuades us of the folly of any who would 'mock the time with fairest show'. If this is characteristically the dramatist's emphasis, drawing upon his deepest sense of the very medium in which he works, in both *Romeo and Juliet* and the last plays there is evident an Elizabethan poet's sense of paradox, of inherent impossibility only to be cancelled when love is triumphant. Romeo's boast—'love-devouring death do what he dare . . .'—and Juliet's defiance of time are not tragic errors. They are not less than statements of the incompatibility between man and time when man would reach beyond time. We must not let our preconceptions blind us to the real drift and emphasis in Shakespeare, more particularly when there are involved ideas of drama and poetry with which we are relatively unfamiliar. That theme of reconciliation which is strongest and most constant of all in Shakespeare has a higher place in the Elizabethan imagination than we ordinarily may be prepared to allow.

> —John Lawlor, *"Romeo and Juliet," Early Shakespeare,* ed. John Russell Brown and Bernard Harris (London: Edward Arnold, 1961), pp. 141–42

❖

John Wain on *Romeo and Juliet* as Comedy

[John Wain (b. 1925), formerly a professor of poetry at Oxford University, is an important modern British poet, novelist, and critic. His critical works include *Essays on Literature and Ideas* (1963) and *A House for Truth* (1973). In this extract from his book on Shakespeare, Wain makes a case for *Romeo and Juliet* as a comedy that turns into a tragedy.]

⟨. . .⟩ where *Hamlet* takes us—albeit stumblingly—into purely tragic territory, the psychological premises of *Romeo and Juliet* are those of the early comedies. Characteristically, those comedies concern themselves with the inborn, unargued stupidity of older people and the life-affirming gaiety and resourcefulness of young ones. The lovers thread their way through obstacles set up by middle-aged vanity and impercipience. Parents are stupid and do not know what is best for their children or themselves: that is a *donnée* and does not have to be justified. *Romeo and Juliet* is in essence a comedy that turns out tragically. That is, it begins with the materials for a comedy—the stupid parental generation, the instant attraction of the young lovers, the quick surface life of street fights, masked balls and comic servants. But this material is blighted. Its gaiety and good fortune are drained away by the fact—also a *donnée*—that the lovers are 'star-crossed'. It is, to that extent, arbitrarily shaped. It is a tragedy because Shakespeare decided to sit down and write a tragedy. It does not build with inherently tragic materials. Where the comedies celebrate order by moving from disharmony to harmony, this play moves from surface disharmony to an almost achieved surface harmony, before being dashed by a blow from its author's fist into fundamental, irremediable disaster.

To put it another way, the form of *Romeo and Juliet* is that of a shattered minuet. The two lovers first come together in a dance (Act I, Scene v), and it is noteworthy that the first words they address to each other are in the form of a sonnet. A dance; a sonnet; these are symbols of a formal, contained wholeness. This wholeness is already threatened. Tybalt has recognized Romeo; and, though his demand for instant combat has been restrained by his host (a rare case of the older generation's being wiser than the younger), he is glowering and planning revenge. The worm is already in the fruit. But the nature of the worm is not explored. The characters move in a certain pattern because the author has decided on that pattern. Romeo and Juliet are all ardour and constancy, their families are all hatred and pride; no one's motives are mixed, and there are no question marks. After the tragedy the survivors are shocked into dropping their vendetta, and Montague and Capulet are united in grief. Once again, there are no question marks. Nothing made them enemies except the clash of their own wills, and nothing is needed to make them brothers except a change of heart.

A good many years went by before Shakespeare again handled this theme of lovers pushed apart by the world. When he did, he was deep in his tragic period, and had long since left behind the simpler notion that suffering is caused solely by the willed actions of human beings. If it were, people would only have to stop behaving tiresomely and paradise would arrive at once.

Romeo and Juliet, wishing to escape from the feud-ridden city of Verona, had planned to make their escape to another city, Padua, and start life anew. The blood-feud that darkened their happiness is seen as an infection as local as a pimple. By travelling a few miles, they can set up in a place where Montague and Capulet cannot reach them. For Troilus and Cressida, this is impossible. The warring camps of Greece and Troy make up their whole world. No one in the play seems to have any consciousness of a wider scene beyond this quarrel. In that respect it is a true Iron-Curtain drama. The unhealed breach divides the world.

—John Wain, The Living World of Shakespeare: A Playgoer's Guide (New York: St. Martin's Press, 1964), pp. 107–8

❖

RAYMOND V. UTTERBACK ON THE DEATH OF MERCUTIO

[Raymond V. Utterback is a former professor at Georgia State University. In this extract, Utterback studies the figure of Mercutio, who almost upstages Romeo as a charismatic figure. Mercutio's death, according to Utterback, is not only a central incident in the play, but it structures the entire work.]

Dr. Johnson did not define the place allotted to Mercutio in the construction of the play, but his suggestion that Mercutio's death be viewed in terms of the play's structure has considerable merit. As the first death represented in the play, it sharply divides the events. Mercutio's death affects the action critically and thoroughly alters the tone of the play. In the midst of the story of romantic love which has occupied the stage, and in spite of the general atmosphere of danger and the predictions of doom, this actual death comes as a shock. It introduces the crucial fact, irrevocable and damaging, that shifts the play into the tragic mode. Before this, despite the various tensions (including those established by the Prologues and the imagery), the events and hopes of several characters are directed toward the reconciliation of the feuding households in love and toward the possible happiness of the lovers. After it, the play moves toward death and the final reconciliation, in grief, of the heirless families. Such happiness as the lovers enjoy after this event and its immediate consequences is but a private moment stolen from an increasingly hostile world. The hopes of recovering their situation and restoring their union are desperate and prove ultimately vain. The consequences attendant upon Mercutio's death directly dominate the third act and reverberate throughout the play. Mercutio's death leads directly to Tybalt's death at Romeo's hands, which in turn becomes the cause of Romeo's banishment, and this, through an intricate chain of contingencies, leads to the final catastrophe. Mercutio's death is thus a primary motivating force for major subsequent events. Furthermore, in the circumstances which lead to it and in the details of the way it is dramatized there appears a pattern which also governs the primary subject of the play, the tragedy of the lovers. ⟨. . .⟩

Mercutio's death is important in the structure of the play for what it leads to; it is a key link in a chain. But it establishes a pattern repeated at other points in the action, and so becomes significant as the primary exhibition of an organizing principle of the play. This pattern comprises, first, a prevailing dramatic situation containing threats, anxieties, dangers, and risks. Shakespeare characteristically made explicit the threatening elements of the situation and placed the spectator in a position to perceive and appreciate the risks. The situation is open, the possibilities for escaping or incurring the risks are both made evident. The overriding condition in Verona is, of course, the opposition of the rival houses and the threat of violent and fatal conflict. At times the violence breaks out, as in the opening scene, but at most times it constitutes a tension that is controlled or at least suppressed. But it provides a constant threatening background against which the characters move. The play receives much of its distinctive character from the sense of threat emanating from this background and the sense that the threat might nevertheless be avoided or overcome. In Mercutio's case the real threat is tangential to the feud; it is personified in Tybalt himself. The risks are intensified by Mercutio's deep personal hostility to Tybalt and his inability to hold his tongue.

Second, a provocation occurs which can actualize threats evident in the dramatic situation. The provocation may be direct and intense, or subtle and implied, but it is a stimulus to the characters, and it triggers the subsequent action. Some provocations do not actually result in violent action, though they tend toward it. Tybalt's address to Mercutio excites the latter, but it does not result in a fight, though perhaps only because the encounter is cut short. Tybalt's insults to Romeo likewise fail to result in the intended clash. Yet the same insults prove an unbearable provocation to Mercutio, and so they result in a fight Tybalt did not intend. The provocations are thus capable of eliciting violence beyond the control and the intentions of those who originate them.

The third element of the pattern is the passionate response to the provocation. Usually there is a sudden and impulsive decision, closely followed by crucial actions. These decisions and actions are made without care or thought for the consequences—and without reflection or judgment. In the scene described above, Mercutio's sudden challenge to Tybalt as "rat-catcher" and the drawing of his sword represent virtually simultaneous decision and action. The tension of the scene is exploited in this rapid movement; one can observe Mercutio's mental and emotional determination, the verbal challenge, and then the physical action in almost the same instant.

Fourth, a tragic consequence follows the passionate action. Tybalt gives Mercutio a fatal wound and escapes unhurt. This result of his challenge elicits great bitterness from Mercutio, who evidently envisaged nothing but his own victory. A little later Romeo conceives of several possible outcomes of his challenge to Tybalt, all of them of tragic import: "Either thou or I, or both, must go with him [Mercutio]" (III.i.128). In this play it quite often seems that the tragic outcome could have been avoided, just as Romeo cannot at first believe that Mercutio's wound is so serious as to cause death. If the Friar's letter had been delivered, or if Romeo had arrived at the tomb only a few moments later, or if Tybalt had not returned to the place where he stabbed Mercutio, or if any of numerous other events had happened only a little differently, the tragic outcome might have been avoided. But the tragic consequences occur, and they speak for themselves.

Finally, the pattern concludes in a blurring of the sense of personal responsibility for the events by a shift of dramatic attention to the impersonal elements of the situation in which the tragic consequences occurred. There is an almost circular movement back to the first element of the pattern. The play moves from an ominous or threatening situation through the decisions of individuals to the limiting contexts in which their decisions and actions took place. This is sometimes dramatized in terms of an individual's blindness to his own role in bringing about disaster. Mercutio complains about the rival houses, but not his own rashness. And other characters in this play have a strong tendency to view the tragic results of a sequence of events and to ignore the process by which those results came about. It is a kind of selective attention operating to emphasize the general and external causes of the events and to minimize the individual and personal responsibilities of the characters.

—Raymond V. Utterback, "The Death of Mercutio," *Shakespeare Quarterly* 24, No. 2 (Spring 1973): 107, 112–13

❖

DERICK R. C. MARSH ON CONVENTIONALITY IN *ROMEO AND JULIET*

[Derick R. C. Marsh (b. 1928), a notable British Shakespeare scholar, is the author of *The Recurring Miracle: A Study of* Cymbeline *and the Last Plays* (1969), *Shakespeare's* Hamlet (1970), and *Passion Lends Them Power: A Study of Shakespeare's Love Tragedies* (1976), from which the following extract is taken. Here, Marsh sees both Romeo and Juliet initially acting in conventional ways—Romeo as the young lover, Juliet as the nubile young woman—but, as the play progresses, they shed these views and achieve distinctive attitudes on life.]

When Romeo himself appears, his enjoyment of his role as the repulsed and love-lorn suitor of Rosaline is very apparent. His speech is extravagant, his paradoxes on the nature of love utterly conventional, his classic cause of disappointment not his rejection because he is the wrong man, but Rosaline's determination to live a life of chastity. In short, as Coleridge noticed, he is presented as a young man ripe to fall in love because he is so much in love with the idea. But when he falls in love with Juliet, he is protected from any charge of infidelity or inconstancy by the very conventional impersonality of his language here, and by the lack of real concern over his state shown by any of his friends, or even by himself. His apostrophes to love carry very little conviction, and his eager readiness to enter into argument with his friends on the subject indicates how little his true sensibilities are engaged. The point, in fact, would appear to be obvious; I have gone on at this length because the criticism that much of Shakespeare's writing in this play has been more concerned with manner than with matter, is, in part, based on these first glimpses of Romeo. Romeo himself, in his readiness to match wits with Mercutio and his friends, is much more concerned with manner than matter, but that is a very different thing. When he sees Juliet and falls in love with her, his starting point may still be this conventional way of thinking and talking about love, but what the play then shows is his progress away from these conventional attitudes to an understanding and an expression of what he really feels.

The introduction of Juliet, too, sees her placed in a thoroughly conventional setting. We first hear of her from her father's disclaimer to Paris of any desire to force her into a too-hasty marriage, or to make her choice of husband for her. From this encounter, and from Juliet's own acceptance of her place as a young girl, the only child of doting parents, watched over by a bawdily garrulous but kind-hearted nurse, there is little to indicate any inclination on her part, or need to go against her parents' wishes. But already attitudes very important for the play's later development are being suggested. It is clear that Paris is regarded as being a very good match by Juliet's parents, and that, in spite of old Capulet's disclaimers and Juliet's own youth, 'It is an honour that I dream not of' is her answer to her mother's question of what she thinks of the prospect of marriage—a man nevertheless is being chosen for her, and this in spite of her mother's own experience of what, on the available evidence, we must assume to have been a not very rewarding marriage made on the same sort of basis. Juliet is old Capulet's only surviving child and he sees her very much as a possession. His pun on earth speaks volumes, while her mother urges Paris' case with a rather more than disinterested force. More even than Romeo, Juliet is being urged to yield to age its traditional prerogative, that it knows better, and must therefore be allowed to choose a course of action for youth.

> —Derick R. C. Marsh, *Passion Lends Them Power: A Study of Shakespeare's Love Tragedies* (Manchester: Manchester University Press, 1976), pp. 54–55

❖

GERRY BRENNER ON FRIAR LAWRENCE

[Gerry Brenner (b. 1937), a professor of English at the University of Montana, has written several books on Ernest Hemingway, including *Concealments on Hemingway's Works* (1983) and The Old Man and the Sea: *Story of a Common Man* (1991). In this extract, Brenner finds that Friar Lawrence is striving for political eminence under the guise of helping the young lovers.]

The most telling proof of Friar Lawrence's political motivation is that he continually oversteps his ecclesiastical functions. By marrying Romeo and Juliet secretly and without parental consent, he knowingly violates strict canon law. He does so not to sanctify an act of Providence that has had Romeo and Juliet fall in love at first sight, but, as his express reason to Romeo indicates, "To turn your households' rancor to pure love." Acting on his own volition and interfering in temporal matters, the friar dramatizes the kind of behavior that so perplexes Capulet's illiterate servant. Trying to determine who is on his master's guest list, he remarks, "It is written that the shoemaker should meddle with his yard and the tailor with his last, the fisher with his pencil and the painter with his nets" (I.ii.39–41). To be sure, the friar is not alone in performing forbidden actions. Tybalt seems to thrive on proscribed behavior. Juliet quickly learns to defy parental dictates. And Romeo is a compulsive gatecrasher, trespassing and committing taboo acts throughout the play. The correlation between the behaviors of the friar and of other characters indicates that excepting Paris, defiance of conventional expectation is wholesale. The correlation also underscores the friar's refusal to abide by God's will. He prefers the autonomy of "My will be done." Taking an active role in the affairs of men, he shows his discontent with leaving matters in the hands of Providence. He even appropriates to himself the task of sending Romeo that crucial letter via a fellow friar, rather than let Romeo's servant, Balthasar, be his emissary, as he had promised Romeo he would (III.iii.169–71).

The friar's herbological interests align him with the play's other drugmaker, the apothecary who commits the outlawed act of selling poison to Romeo. But those interests are more tellingly the means by which Shakespeare has the friar flagrantly expose his urge for political preeminence. The clergy were, of course, usually conversant with simple natural medicine. And the friar's interest in alchemy surely has its beneficial aspect. But his chemical expertise shows that like many a scientific meddler, he tampers with God's natural order and uses nature's secret powers to serve his own purposes. More specifically, on the pretext of restoring the lovers to each other, he tells a distraught Juliet that the ultimate consequence of her drinking his potion will be that Romeo will "bear thee hence to Mantua" (IV.i.117). But why is his alchemy necessary? Why not simply help Juliet flee Verona if he is genuinely interested in reuniting the lovers? His elaborate ruse requires that Juliet deceive her family, that they suffer unnecessary grief, and that he dissemble before them. More, his ruse tells us that he is less concerned with the lovers' happiness than with his ambition. That is, though the play never explicitly considers the question, it implicitly asks us to inquire: What would have happened had his ruse been successful?

Is my question beyond the scope of the play? I think not. After all, the recurrent motif of haste in the play sweeps the plot ever into the future. Capulet eagerly looks forward to Juliet's marriage, as does Paris. Prince Escalus eagerly looks forward to the day when the feud will be over. Romeo and Juliet eagerly look forward to being reunited. And Friar Lawrence eagerly looks forward, I believe, to a brilliant scenario. Had his ruse worked, he could have called for an audience with the prince—the Montagues and Capulets in attendance, naturally. Then he could have informed the Capulets that their daughter was not dead, as they thought, but was alive and happy. He could have explained that his sleeping potion—"(so tutored by my art)" (V.iii.243)—had made her appear dead. And he could have expected that Capulet would rejoice, just as he had after the friar had presumably taught Juliet to defer to his will and so to marry Paris: "My heart is wondrous light, / Since this same wayward girl is so reclaim'd" (IV.ii.46–47). The friar could then have informed all present of the end that his resurrection scheme served: to end the feud and so restore civil harmony by marrying Romeo and Juliet. However humbly he might have divulged his gospel, its effect would be the same. He would receive civil adulation, such praise as Capulet had earlier accorded him: "Now, afore God, this reverend holy friar, / All our whole city is much bound to him" (IV.ii.31–32). And such praise would vault the friar over the prince as Verona's miracle worker, its true leader.

—Gerry Brenner, "Shakespeare's Politically Ambitious Friar,"
Shakespeare Studies 13 (1980): 53–54

❖

JULIA KRISTEVA ON THE DARKER ELEMENTS IN *ROMEO AND JULIET*

[Julia Kristeva (b. 1941) is a Bulgarian-born French novelist, linguist, psychoanalyst, and literary theorist. Her publications include *Essays in Semiotics* (1971), *Polylogue* (1977), and *Desire in Language* (1980). In this extract, Kristeva argues that the obvious romantic tone of *Romeo and Juliet* is undermined by the darker emotion of hatred.]

One often likens Romeo and Juliet as a couple to Tristam and Isolde, producing the evidence of a love thwarted by social rules; emphasizing how the couple is cursed and destroyed by Christianity, which smothers passion at the heart of marriage; seeking a revelation of the death that rules at the core of amatory jouissance. Shakespeare's text includes, with all that, an even more corrosive element, which his skill with ambiguity and the reversal of values handles with insidious magic in the very height of the most intense glorification of love. Under the guise of sex, it is hatred that prevails, and that comes out most obviously in the very first pages of the text. In the first scene, the two servants' remarks, peppered with puns and obscenities, cause the darkness of sex and inversions of all sorts to hang over this presumably pure romance. One is already prepared for Romeo's remark terming love 'a madness most discreet' (I, i, 192), even saying that 'it is too rough, too rude, too boisterous, and it pricks like thorn' (I, iv, 25–6). A little later it will be described by Mercutio—a baneful character who, along with Benvolio, brings about a chain of violence and whose death in the third act forces Romeo to avenge him by killing Tybalt—by means of the allegory of the fairies' midwife, Queen Mab. A gnomelike ghost, fascinating and hideous, ruler of amorous bodies, the dark, drunken, and murderous other side of loving radiance, it is Queen Mab who calls the tune with 'her whip of cricket's bone; the lash, of film' (I, iv, 63).

It is Juliet, however, who finds the most intense expressions to show that this love is supported by hatred. One could possibly see in the words of this noble maiden a simple rhetorical device at once heralding a final death, or an ambiguous language clause, blending opposites, something that is operative at other moments of the play and in Shakespeare's esthetics in general. But more deeply, what is involved is hatred at the very origin on the amorous surge. A hatred that antedates the veil of amorous idealization. Let us note that it is a woman, Juliet, who is most immediately unconscious of it, senses it with a sleepwalker's lucidity. Thus, as early as their first meeting—while Romeo suddenly forgets Rosaline, whose love nevertheless tortured him sorely a short time before, and only admits 'The more is my unrest' when he is told Juliet is the daughter of the enemy family—it is Juliet herself who states frankly, 'My only love sprung from my only hate!' (I, v, 139).

Did not Romeo himself, however, go to the Capulets' feast knowing that he was going to a feast of hatred? Juliet, again: 'Tis but thy name that is my enemy' (II, ii, 38). Or else, at the very height of the amatory monologue that sets in place the passion of waiting and extols the lovers' qualities ('Come, night, come, Romeo, thou day in night . . .'), Juliet continues innocently, 'come, gentle night . . . and, when he shall die, take him and cut him out in little stars, and he will make the face of heaven so fine, that all the world will be in love with the night . . .' (III, ii, 19–24). 'When he shall die, take him and cut him out': it is as if one heard a discreet version of the Japanese *Realm of the Senses.* That feeling goes unnoticed because it is swept along by a hatred that one can look in the eye—the familial, social curse is more respectable and bearable than the unconscious hatred of the lovers for each other. The fact remains that Juliet's jouissance is often stated through the anticipation—the desire?—of Romeo's death. This, long before her drugged sleep deceives Romeo and leads him to suicide, long before she turns that death wish back upon herself at the sight of Romeo's corpse, driving herself to suicide, too: 'Methinks I see thee, now thou art below, as one dead in the bottom of a tomb' (III, v, 55–6).

Such frequent evocations of death are not simply intended to state that there is no room for passion in the world of old people, and, more generally, in marriage—that love must die on the threshold of its legislation, that eros and the law are incompatible. Friar Lawrence says it indeed, and this is a leftover from vulgarized Christian asceticism: 'She's not well married that lives married long, but she's best married that dies married young' (IV, v, 77–8).

More deeply, more passionately, we are dealing with the intrinsic presence of hatred in amatory feeling itself. In the object relation, the relation with an *other,* hatred, as Freud said, is more ancient than love. As soon as an other appears different from myself, it becomes alien, repelled, repugnant, abject—hated. Even hallucinating love, as distinct from auto-erotic satisfaction, as a precocious feeling of narcissistic fulfillment in which the other is not sharply separated from myself, does not otherwise come up in relation to that other until later, through the capacity for primary idealization. But as soon as the strength of desire that is joined with love sets the integrity of the self ablaze; as soon as it breaks down its solidity through the drive-impelled torrent of passion, hatred—the primary bench mark of object relation—emerges out of repression. Eroticized according to the variants of sadomasochism, or coldly dominant in more lasting relationships that have already exhausted the delights of infidelity, as delusive as it is seductive, hatred is the keynote in the couple's passionate melody. Whether heterosexual or homosexual, the couple is the utopic wager that paradise lost can be made lasting—but perhaps it is merely desired and truly never known?—the paradise of loving understanding between the child and its parents. The child, male or female, hallucinates its merging with a nourishing-mother-and-ideal-father, in short a conglomeration that already condenses two into one. That child, the loving child, in its couple mania, tries to make two where there were three. Man or woman, when he or she aspires to be a couple, the lover goes through the mirage of being the 'husband' or 'wife' or an ideal father: that is the extent to which the idealized object of love dons the finery of that 'father of individual prehistory' Freud talked about, the one who absorbs those delightful primary identifications. In such a coupling with the ideal, shored up by a happy, domesticated fatherhood, man becomes feminized; is there anything more androgynous, or even feminine, than the adolescent madly in love with an adolescent of the opposite sex? One soon notices, however, in the last instance (that is, if the couple truly becomes one, if it lasts), that each of the protagonists, he and she, has married, through the other, his or her mother.

—Julia Kristeva, "Romeo and Juliet: Love-Hatred in the Couple," Tales of Love (1983), tr. Leon S. Roudiez (New York: Columbia University Press, 1987), pp. 220–23

❖

EDWARD SNOW ON LANGUAGE AND FEMALE SUBSERVIENCE IN
ROMEO AND JULIET

[Edward Snow is a professor of English at Rice University and the translator of Rainer Maria Rilke's *New Poems* (1984) and *The Book of Images* (1991). In this extract, Snow maintains that the language of *Romeo and Juliet* emphasizes women's subservient place in the social hierarchy.]

Romeo and Juliet is full of a sense of how social prerogatives based on the oppression of women place the men who enjoy them at a disadvantage in the realm of primary experience. Sampson reasons that since "women, being the weaker vessels, are ever thrust to the wall," he will "push Montague's men from the wall, and thrust his maids to the wall" (1.1.15–18), even though he himself has just admitted that the place nearest the wall is the superior position. And the image of the maid thrust against the wall by Sampson's gross assaults, the object not even of sexual lust but deflected male rivalry, is somehow balanced by that of the Nurse "Sitting in the sun under the dove-house wall," alone with Juliet In the world of women, enjoying there the backing of an elemental realm whose existence Sampson, with his insecure phallic readiness to give and take offence, will never even remotely intuit. Mercutio, for whom the "sociable" is an antidote to "groaning for love" (2.4.88–89), likewise perceives woman's position in love as analogous to her position in the civil order, and the sexual act as a means of subduing her to it: "This is the hag, when maids lie on their backs, / That presses them and learns them first to bear, / Making them women of good carriage" (1.4.92–94). Yet the bearing women are expected to endure in society is matched in the realm of ontological experience by a *power* to bear, and bear fruit, that men are denied by a code that regards submission as "dishonorable [and] vile" (as Mercutio terms Romeo's "calm" reaction to Tybalt's challenge), and defines freedom as a matter of keeping one's neck "out of collar" (1.1.4–5). Juliet's apostrophe to night suggests, moreover, that woman's sexual place is where the imagination thrives. The climax of her speech sublimates an intoxicating sensation of floating weightlessly in a void that encompasses the sexual act, while at the same time being oneself its ground and bearing the whole of it ("For thou wilt lie upon the wings of night / Whiter than new snow upon a raven's back"), that seems accessible only from beneath. She is the one in a position to take in sexual experience, and witness the epiphany that occurs at the moment of relinquishment: "Give me my Romeo, and, when I shall die, / Take him and cut him out in little stars, / And he will make the face of heaven so fine . . ." Romeo's imagination, by contrast, does not seem open to the sexual act in the way Juliet's is, and though his experience in love can't be reduced to Mercutio's travesty of it as "a great natural that runs lolling up and down to hide his bauble in a hole" (2.4.91–93), its horizons do seem limited by his desire to rest in Juliet's breast.

Similar ironies govern the socially instituted discrepancy between Romeo's and Juliet's approaches to love. We first encounter Romeo not being addressed by the "intergenerational" will of the Montague family (as we might expect had Shakespeare wished either to portray the love relationship as symmetrical or explore it primarily within the division between the two families), but adrift in the unsupervised realm of male adolescence. Yet the liberty to "inquire" he enjoys there has resulted in a mind full of knowledge about love (obviously acquired, as Juliet remarks, "by th' book") that betrays the absence of any felt connection with the source of instinctual wisdom Juliet draws from. He also enjoys a freedom of movement and the company and support of friends, while she is confined within the family places (hall, bedroom, tomb) and isolated from anyone with whom she might share her experiences as a young woman. But as a result she is the one who seems most capable and at home in the solitude that is love's element ("My dismal scene I needs must act alone"), and the one who provides the impetus and inner direction of their relationship once Romeo initiates it. His social advantages also create transitional conflicts that Juliet is spared. The male bonds that form in adolescence involve phallic allegiances against women and the threats of impotence, emasculation, and effeminacy posed by the actual sexual relation—hence Mercutio's almost compulsive eagerness to generate collective sexual ridicule of the Nurse, and his mockery of a "fishified"

Romeo ("without his roe, like a dried herring") who is only "Romeo" (Mercutio insists) when he is "sociable" and not "groaning for love." These attitudes persist, moreover—as the opening scene makes clear—in the adult world, and hence make the conflict Mercutio articulates between social identity and sexual relatedness not just a passing adolescent stage but a permanent male dilemma. Romeo is of all Shakespeare's romantic or tragic heroes the one least inhibited by these male bonds and the cultural values that reinforce them. When the play opens he is already disaffected with society, and too narcissistically self-absorbed to feel the *pull* of friendship. And when he falls in love with Juliet, he positively relishes the submissive role of fitting himself to her will. Yet Mercutio has to die (so the plot seems to tell us) before Romeo and Juliet's relationship can be sexually consummated, and Mercutio himself blames his death on Romeo's betrayal—for "coming between" Mercutio and Tybalt, to be sure, but also, one feels, for allowing something to come between the two of them. Shakespeare thus manages to make the presence of a bad conscience about sexual love that is endemic to masculinity felt in the background of Romeo's experience, and the one short moment that Romeo falls back into it plunges him and the entire play into tragedy: "O sweet Juliet, / Thy beauty hath made me effeminate, / And in my temper soft'ned valor's steel" (3.1.113–15).

—Edward Snow, "Language and Sexual Difference in *Romeo and Juliet,*" *Shakespeare's "Rough Magic": Renaissance Essays in Honor of C. L. Barber,* ed. Peter Erickson and Coppélia Kahn (Newark: University of Delaware Press, 1985), pp. 185–86

❖

CEDRIC WATTS ON THE SOURCES FOR *ROMEO AND JULIET*

[Cedric Watts is a professor of English at the University of Texas. He has written *The Deceptive Text: An Introduction to Covert Plots* (1984), *A Preface to Keats* (1985), and a study of *Hamlet* (1988). In this extract from his book on *Romeo and Juliet,* Watts traces the sources of the play to works from classical antiquity to Brooke's *Romeus and Juliet,* showing how Shakespeare improved upon his sources through skillful dramatic construction.]

In the second century AD, the *Ephesiaca* by Xenophon of Ephesus tells how two teenagers, Anthia and Habrocomes, fall in love at first sight and subsequently marry. Anthia becomes separated from her husband and is rescued from robbers by one Perilaus, who himself then seeks to marry her. To evade this second marriage, Anthia bribes a needy physician to supply her with a potion to enable her to commit suicide; but he, scrupulously, supplies not a poison but a soporific. On her bridal day she drinks it, swoons, is thought dead and is interred in a tomb; later, she awakens there and is carried away by tomb-robbers. Habrocomes learns of Anthia's apparent death and interment, and hastens to the tomb; after many vicissitudes he and Anthia are at last reunited.

There is a consensus among commentators that Shakespeare had no direct knowledge of the *Ephesiaca*; what is evident is that it represents an intermediate stage between those ancient resurrection myths and the subsequent tales which were studied by Shakespeare. Xenophon helped to transmit the 'apparent death' or *Scheintod* motif (already established in legends like those of Eurydice and Alcestis) as well as the interlinked motifs of 'death as lover, tomb as bridal chamber' which had appeared in Sophocles' *Antigone,* Petronius' *Satyricon,* Apuleius' *Metamorphoses,* Achilles Tatius' *Leucippe and Clitophon* and Heliodorus' *Ethiopian Story,* and which modern opera-lovers encounter in Verdi's *Aïda.*

By the fifteenth century, the plot had already accumulated more of the features now familiar to us. The *Cinquante Novelle* of Masuccio Salernitano (Naples, 1476), includes the story of Mariotto and Giannozza of Siena. These two lovers are secretly married by a Friar. Mariotto then quarrels with a citizen, kills him, and is banished. Giannozza's irascible father urges her to marry a suitor he has chosen; so, after sending a message to forewarn her husband of her plan, she takes a sleeping potion provided by the Friar, is thought dead and is entombed. The Friar releases her, and she sails to Alexandria in the hope of meeting Mariotto there. But her message has not reached him, for the messenger has been captured by pirates. Hearing that she has died, Mariotto returns home and, while attempting to open the tomb, is arrested. He is beheaded, and Giannozza consequently dies of grief.

A subsequent version by Luigi da Porto transfers the events to Verona, renames the lovers 'Romeo' and 'Giulietta', specifies a feud between their two families (the Montecchi and the Cappelletti), and says that Romeo met Giulietta when he went to a ball in the hope of seeing a lady who had repulsed his courtship. After the clandestine marriage to Giulietta, which Friar Lorenzo hopes will unite the feuding families, Romeo kills one Thebaldo and flees to Mantua. Giulietta takes the sleeping potion to avoid marriage to a suitor, a count, who is favoured by her father. Friar Lorenzo's message to Romeo is entrusted to another Friar who fails to deliver it, as Romeo is absent. Romeo, meanwhile, hearing that she is dead, has gone to the tomb and taken poison; Giulietta awakens, speaks with him and embraces him; he dies; and she commits suicide—by holding her breath! The parents, on learning of the circumstances, are reconciled, and the feud ends.

The tale was then transmitted and elaborated by Bandello, Boaistuau and various adaptors, acquiring a conspiratorial nurse, a culpable apothecary, and other familiar features. Eventually it became Arthur Brooke's long narrative poem, *The Tragicall Historye of Romeus and Juliet* (1562), and this was Shakespeare's main source. ⟨. . .⟩

In converting the narrative into a play, Shakespeare has given direct physicality, movement, colour, vitality and a diversity of modes of eloquence in poetry and prose to what formerly was relatively inert: everywhere there is new life, intelligence and questing cogency. Contrasts in discourse, characterisation, tone and scene are repeatedly introduced or accentuated. In Brooke, the time-scale of events is vague but lengthy: at least nine months elapse. In Shakespeare, the time-scale is dramatically compressed to just four days (from Sunday to Thursday morning), so that the momentum is impetuously rapid. Furthermore, this momentum is given thematic force, for one of the main themes then becomes the attraction and danger of impetuous action. The love-relationship gains the intensity and poignacy of precipitate brevity. And Shakespeare not only enlivens the structure but also co-ordinates it very systematically. Brooke's poem began with a sonnet summarising the plot; Shakespeare places a summarising sonnet at the beginning not only of Act 1 but also of Act 2, and (with superbly symbolic use of poetic form) lets the first exchange of Romeo and Juliet blend into a formally perfect sonnet. In Brooke the feud is presented with relative vagueness as a matter in the background of the main action until the killing which leads to Romeus's banishment; Shakespeare boldly foregrounds the feud first at the outset, second near the midpoint (Act 3 Scene 1, after which the Prince banishes Romeo), and third at the conclusion, so that the contrast between the private and the public, the intimate and the political, becomes much more prominent and forceful. The play's profusion of minor characters (Abram, Balthasar, Peter, Sampson, Gregory, Potpan, Anthony, etc.) also helps to establish as significant realities the social and political contexts.

> —Cedric Watts, *Romeo and Juliet* (Boston: Twayne, 1991), pp. 15–17, 19

❖

LEAH SCRAGG ON *ROMEO AND JULIET* AND *ANTONY AND CLEOPATRA*

[Leah Scragg is the author of *Discovering Shakespeare's Meaning* (1987) and *Shakespeare's Mouldy Tales* (1992), from which the following extract is taken. Here, Scragg compares *Romeo and Juliet* with *Antony and Cleopatra,* both of which feature the suicide of the hero as a result of a false report of the death of the hero's lover.]

Romeo and Juliet (1594–96) and *Antony and Cleopatra* (1606–07), the two plays in which a hypothetical death appears in a tragic context, offer the simplest approach to the exploration of the motif. At first glance, the two works have much in common. Both enact the tragic process arising from the passionate attachment between a pair of lovers in a divided world. Romeo and Juliet are separated by the feud between their families, Antony and Cleopatra by the irreconcilable oppositions between the societies to which they belong. The hero of both tragedies commits suicide as a result of a false report that his mistress is dead, while the heroine takes her own life as a result of her lover's death. Moreover, in both tragedies the feigned death of the heroine is productive of a sense of waste, in that the tragic outcome is not felt by the audience to be inevitable. Romeo kills himself at the very moment that Juliet begins to waken from her drugged sleep, while Antony receives his death wound only seconds before learning that Cleopatra is alive. In both cases, the superior awareness of the theatre audience imposes a distance between those outside the play world and the central figures. Rather than being wholly involved in the hero's anguish, the spectator is agonizingly aware of his mistake, and is engaged on one level in willing him to delay his action in the hope that the truth will be revealed.

Nevertheless, for all the superficial similarities between the two structures, the plays draw on different sources and constitute very different kinds of dramatic experience. As noted in the previous chapter, *Romeo and Juliet* looks back to Brooke's *The Tragicall Historye of Romeus and Juliet,* a tale designed, according to the author, to exhibit 'a coople of unfortunate lovers, thralling themselves to unhonest desire, neglecting the authoritie and advise of parents and frendes, conferring their principall counsels with dronken gossyppes, and superstitious friers . . . finallye, by all meanes of unhonest lyfe, hastyng to most unhappye deathe'. Shakespeare remains faithful to Brooke's narrative throughout, but he does not embrace its moral judgements, transforming what purports to be an exemplary 'history' into a tragedy of doomed love. The closing scene of the play is generally regarded as among the most poignant in the dramatist's work. Prevented from acknowledging their attachment, the lovers have married in secret, but are obliged to part after a single night together when Romeo is banished for killing Tybalt. Threatened with a second marriage, Juliet swallows a potion that induces a death-like sleep, but the letter informing Romeo of her intention fails to reach him, and he mistakenly supposes her to be dead. Making his way to her family vault he takes poison as she is about to regain consciousness, while she, finding his body beside her when she wakens, kills herself with his dagger.

The painful nature of this last scene clearly depends in large measure upon the awareness of the theatre audience that Juliet is not dead as Romeo believes, and that a tragic outcome could be averted. The fate of the couple is not presented as the inescapable product of a depraved life, the interpretation Brooke's 'To the Reader' invites, but as a consequence of a series of accidents, in that had Romeo received the letter, or Juliet awakened a moment earlier, the strategem would have been a success. The role of chance rather than character in determining the fate of the lovers is integral, moreover, to the pattern of action that the drama as a whole enacts. The relationship between events is fortuitous rather than inevitable, while the fates of the dramatis personae are governed not by intention, or by the moral order, but by chance. It is chance that the lovers belong to rival families, chance that Mercutio dies through Romeo's agency, and chance that Romeo himself becomes the instrument of Tybalt's death.

—Leah Scragg, *Shakespeare's Mouldy Tales: Recurrent Plot Motifs in Shakespearean Drama* (London: Longman, 1992), pp. 159–60

❖

D. Douglas Waters on Catharsis in *Romeo and Juliet*

[D. Douglas Waters (b. 1929) is a professor of English at the University of Wisconsin at Eau Claire and author of *Duessa as Theological Satire* (1970) and *Christian Settings in Shakespeare's Tragedies* (1994), from which the following extract is taken. Here, Waters argues that the catharsis or purgation that defines classic tragedy is, in *Romeo and Juliet,* experienced by the audience rather than by the characters in the play.]

⟨. . .⟩ how and in what sense does catharsis as clarification of human experience work in *Romeo and Juliet*? Instead of demanding that the tragic figures learn moral values from mistakes in making moral choices (as the old purgation theory of catharsis has often demanded) catharsis as clarification simply suggests that we as the audience learn from the experience of the whole *mimesis* or dramatic representation without the insistence that the characters in the plot learn as much as we do. The common element in tragedies is not the cognitive experience of the tragic characters but the audience's cognitive experience based on pity and fear for the tragic hero and/or heroine. So trying to determine whether or not Romeo and Juliet ever know for sure what hit them or whether or not they learn much about their wrong choices is trying to look through the wrong end of the telescope. If I am right here and if my interpretation of fate in the play is right, then perhaps we can understand the tragic power of our catharsis as intellectual, moral, and emotional clarification in *Romeo and Juliet*. It is our painful awareness that the lovers are destroyed by fate as a mysterious cosmic force working through the external circumstances of the feud. As we follow Shakespeare's tragic *mimesis,* his presentation of the whole chain of events the way that he imaginatively views the world while in the creation of the play itself, we become engaged in a pleasing process that is pleasing because it is also a learning process. Learning through the incidences of the plot and becoming involved in them intellectually, morally, and emotionally are all part of our overall response, our catharsis as clarification or enlightenment based on our pity and fear for the tragic characters, their experiences, and their reactions. Our intellectual clarification is our understanding that fate is so against the lovers that—do what they would or what the priest and the nurse would—nothing but their death could destroy their parents' feud (strife). Our moral clarification or enlightenment or cognition is our feeling or intuition that, by the time we reach the last scene, the lovers are not thwarted by any dishonesty or ill intention on their part, though they are not perfect but are inexperienced human beings who are innocent of any incorrect moral choice. In this context it would be perverse to say Shakespeare failed to produce what he did not try to produce. The lovers are not destroyed by lust (desire, whether innocent or otherwise) nor by love (idealistic or otherwise). So part of our catharsis as moral clarification is our recognition that, far from their doing anything that would deserve complete failure to live together, all they really hope for is to be together; our catharsis as moral clarification is the intuitive insight that the lovers themselves did nothing that led fate to drive iron wedges between them. Our catharsis as emotional clarification is experienced throughout the tragic *mimesis* in the situations that arouse our pity and fear for the lovers. Only a few examples are needed here. We pity the lovers when Romeo is banished, when Juliet drinks the sleeping potion, and when Romeo gets the false message about her death, buys poison, goes to her grave, and drinks it *before* the priest arrives and *before* Juliet awakes; they deserve none of these quirks of fate. Our fear for them is aroused and intensified in that, given the full unfolding evidence in the whole mimetic process, they are people like ourselves neither completely evil nor completely good and if fate does destroy someone like them then it could, at least imaginatively and conceivably, destroy us. This is the frightful and mysterious part of the whole tragedy. We need not in our own outlook be fatalistic to appreciate tragedies of fate; but, it seems, we must be imaginatively willing to look at the world in this way as we are responding to this type of play. As I have suggested, then, the play is a tragedy of fate and a very successful one at that. Only if we demand *a priori* that tragedy be of only one kind— tragedy of character—can we pretend that the workings of fate, fortune, and accident disqualify *Romeo and Juliet* as a tragedy.

—D. Douglas Waters, *Christian Settings in Shakespeare's Tragedies* (London: Associated University Presses, 1994), pp. 138–40

❖

Books by
William Shakespeare

Venus and Adonis. 1593.

The Rape of Lucrece. 1594.

Henry VI. 1594.

Titus Andronicus. 1594.

The Taming of the Shrew. 1594.

Romeo and Juliet. 1597.

Richard III. 1597.

Richard II. 1597.

Love's Labour's Lost. 1598.

Henry IV. 1598.

The Passionate Pilgrim. 1599.

A Midsummer Night's Dream. 1600.

The Merchant of Venice. 1600.

Much Ado about Nothing. 1600.

Henry V. 1600.

The Phoenix and the Turtle. 1601.

The Merry Wives of Windsor. 1602.

Hamlet. 1603.

King Lear. 1608.

Troilus and Cressida. 1609.

Sonnets. 1609.

Pericles. 1609.

Othello. 1622.

Mr. William Shakespeares Comedies, Histories & Tragedies.
Ed. John Heminge and Henry Condell. 1623 (First Folio),
1632 (Second Folio), 1663 (Third Folio), 1685 (Fourth Folio).

Poems. 1640.

Works. Ed. Nicholas Rowe. 1709. 6 vols.

Works. Ed. Alexander Pope. 1723–25. 6 vols.

Works. Ed. Lewis Theobald. 1733. 7 vols.

Works. Ed. Thomas Hanmer. 1743–44. 6 vols.

Works. Ed. William Warburton. 1747. 8 vols.

Plays. Ed. Samuel Johnson. 1765. 8 vols.

Plays and Poems. Ed. Edmond Malone. 1790. 10 vols.

The Family Shakespeare. Ed. Thomas Bowdler. 1807. 4 vols.

Works. Ed. J. Payne Collier. 1842–44. 8 vols.

Works. Ed. H. N. Hudson. 1851–56. 11 vols.

Works. Ed. Alexander Dyce. 1857. 6 vols.

Works. Ed. Richard Grant White. 1857–66. 12 vols.

Works (Cambridge Edition). Ed. William George Clark, John
Glover, and William Aldis Wright. 1863–66. 9 vols.

A New Variorum Edition of the Works of Shakespeare.
Ed. H. H. Furness et al. 1871– .

Works. Ed. W. J. Rolfe. 1871–96. 40 vols.

The Pitt Press Shakespeare. Ed. A. W. Verity. 1890–1905.
13 vols.

The Warwick Shakespeare. 1893–1938. 13 vols.

The Temple Shakespeare. Ed. Israel Gollancz. 1894–97.
40 vols.

The Arden Shakespeare. Ed. W. J. Craig, R. H. Case et al. 1899–1924. 37 vols.

The Shakespeare Apocrypha. Ed. C. F. Tucker Brooke. 1908.

The Yale Shakespeare. Ed. Wilbur L. Cross, Tucker Brooke, and Willard Highley Durham. 1917–27. 40 vols.

The New Shakespeare (Cambridge Edition). Ed. Arthur Quiller-Couch and John Dover Wilson. 1921–62. 38 vols.

The New Temple Shakespeare. Ed. M. R. Ridley. 1934–36. 39 vols.

Works. Ed. George Lyman Kittredge. 1936.

The Penguin Shakespeare. Ed. G. B. Harrison. 1937–59. 36 vols.

The New Clarendon Shakespeare. Ed. R. E. C. Houghton. 1938– .

The Arden Shakespeare. Ed. Una Ellis-Fermor et al. 1951– .

The Complete Pelican Shakespeare. Ed. Alfred Harbage. 1969.

The Complete Signet Classic Shakespeare. Ed. Sylvan Barnet. 1972.

The Oxford Shakespeare. Ed. Stanley Wells. 1982– .

The New Cambridge Shakespeare. Ed. Philip Brockbank. 1984– .

Works about William Shakespeare and *Romeo and Juliet*

Adams, Barry B. "The Prudence of Prince Escalus." *ELH* 35 (1968): 32–50.

Andreas, James. "The Neutering of *Romeo and Juliet*." In *Ideological Approaches to Shakespeare: The Practice of Theory*, ed. Robert P. Merrix. Lewiston, NY: Edwin Mellen Press, 1992, pp. 229–42.

Andrews, John F., ed. Romeo and Juliet: *Critical Essays*. New York: Garland, 1993.

Belsey, Catherine. "The Name of the Rose in *Romeo and Juliet*." *Yearbook of English Studies* 23 (1993): 125–42.

Bentley, Greg. "Poetics of Power: Money as Sign and Substance in *Romeo and Juliet*." *Explorations in Renaissance Culture* 17 (1991): 145–66.

Black, James. "The Visual Artistry of *Romeo and Juliet*." *Studies in English Literature 1500–1900* 15 (1975): 245–56.

Bowling, Lawrence E. "The Thematic Framework of *Romeo and Juliet*." *PMLA* 64 (1949): 208–20.

Bryant, J. C. "The Problematic Friar in *Romeo and Juliet*." *English Studies* 55 (1974): 340–50.

Cain, H. Howard. "*Romeo and Juliet:* A Reinterpretation." *Shakespeare Association Bulletin* 22 (1947): 163–92.

Carroll, William T. " 'We Were Born to Die': *Romeo and Juliet*." *Comparative Drama* 15 (1981): 54–71.

Chang, Joseph S. M. J. "The Language of Paradox in *Romeo and Juliet*." *Shakespeare Studies* 3 (1967): 22–42.

Charlton, Henry B. "*Romeo and Juliet* as an Experimental Tragedy." *Proceedings of the British Academy* 25 (1939): 143–85.

Cribb, T. J. "The Unity of *Romeo and Juliet.*" *Shakespeare Survey* 34 (1981): 93–104.

Driver, Tom F. "The Shakespearean Clock: Time and the Vision of Reality in *Romeo and Juliet* and *The Tempest.*" *Shakespeare Quarterly* 15 (1964): 363–70.

Estrin, Barbara L. "Romeo, Juliet, and the Art of Naming Love." *Ariel* 12, No. 2 (April 1981): 31–49.

Evans, Bertrand. "The Brevity of Friar Laurence." *PMLA* 65 (1950): 841–65.

Evans, Robert O. *The Osier Cage: Rhetorical Devices in* Romeo and Juliet. Lexington: University Press of Kentucky, 1966.

Everett, Barbara. "*Romeo and Juliet:* The Nurse's Story." *Critical Quarterly* 14 (1972): 129–39.

Faber, M. D. "The Adolescent Suicide of Romeo and Juliet." *Psychoanalytic Review* 59 (1972): 169–82.

Farrell, Kirby. "Love, Death, and Patriarchy in *Romeo and Juliet.*" In *Shakespeare's Personality,* ed. Norman N. Holland, Sidney Homan, and Bernard J. Paris. Berkeley: University of California Press, 1989, pp. 86–102.

Holmer, Joan Ozark. " 'Myself Condemned and Myself Excus'd': Tragic Effects in *Romeo and Juliet.*" *Studies in Philology* 88 (1991): 345–62.

Hosley, Richard. "The Use of the Upper Stage in *Romeo and Juliet.*" *Shakespeare Quarterly* 5 (1954): 371–79.

Jones, Barry. "*Romeo and Juliet:* The Genesis of a Classic." In *Italian Storytellers: Essays on Italian Narrative Literature,* ed. Eric Haywood and Cormac O'Cuilleanain. Dublin: Irish Academic Press, 1989, pp. 150–81.

Laird, David. "The Generation of Style in *Romeo and Juliet.*" *Journal of English and Germanic Philology* 63 (1964): 204–13.

Levenson, Jill L. "The Definition of Love: Shakespeare's Phrasing in *Romeo and Juliet.*" *Shakespeare Studies* 15 (1982): 21–36.

―――――. "Romeo and Juliet Before Shakespeare." *Studies in Philology* 81 (1984): 325–47.

Levin, Harry. "Form and Formality in *Romeo and Juliet*." *Shakespeare Quarterly* 11 (1960): 1–11.

McArthur, Herbert. "Romeo's Loquacious Friend." *Shakespeare Quarterly* 10 (1959): 35–44.

Moisan, Thomas. " 'O Any Thing, Of Nothing, First Create!': Gender and Patriarchy and the Tragedy of *Romeo and Juliet*." In *In Another Country: Feminist Perspectives on Renaissance Drama*, ed. Dorothea Kehler and Susan Baker. Metuchen, NJ: Scarecrow Press, 1991, pp. 113–36.

―――――. "Rhetoric and the Rehearsal of Death: The 'Lamentations' Scene in *Romeo and Juliet*." *Shakespeare Quarterly* 34 (1983): 390–404.

Moore, Olin H. *The Legend of* Romeo and Juliet. Columbus: Ohio State University Press, 1950.

Munns, Jessica. " 'The Dark Disorders of a Divided State': Otway and Shakespeare's *Romeo and Juliet*." *Comparative Drama* 19 (1985–86): 347–62.

Myers, Jeffrey Raynors. "Ut Picturae Poemata." *Renaissance Papers*, 1987, pp. 71–93.

Nevo, Ruth. "Tragic Form in *Romeo and Juliet*." *Studies in English Literature 1500–1900* 9 (1969): 241–58.

Parker, Douglas H. "Light and Dark Imagery in *Romeo and Juliet*." *Queen's Quarterly* 75 (1968): 663–74.

Porter, Joseph A. *Shakespeare's Mercutio: His History and Drama*. Chapel Hill: University of North Carolina Press, 1988.

Ryan, Kiernan. "*Romeo and Juliet:* The Language of Tragedy." In *The Taming of the Text: Explorations in Language, Literature and Culture*, ed. Willie van Peer. London: Routledge, 1988, pp. 106–21.

Seward, James H. *Tragic Vision in* Romeo and Juliet. Washington, DC: Consortium Press, 1973.

Siegel, Paul N. "Christianity and the Religion of Love in *Romeo and Juliet*." *Shakespeare Quarterly* 12 (1961): 371–92.

Smith, Gordon Ross. "The Balance of Themes in *Romeo and Juliet.*" In *Essays on Shakespeare,* ed. Gordon Ross Smith. University Park: Pennsylvania State University Press, 1965, pp. 15–66.

Snyder, Susan. "*Romeo and Juliet:* Comedy into Tragedy." *Essays in Criticism* 20 (1970): 391–402.

Stamm, R. "The First Meeting of the Lovers in Shakespeare's *Romeo and Juliet.*" *English Studies* 67 (1986): 2–13.

Stevens, Martin. "Juliet's Nurse: Love's Herald." *Papers on Language and Literature* 2 (1966): 195–206.

Stone, George W. "*Romeo and Juliet:* The Source of Its Modern Stage Career." *Shakespeare Quarterly* 15 (1964): 191–206.

Tanselle, G. Thomas. "Time in *Romeo and Juliet.*" *Shakespeare Quarterly* 15 (1964): 349–61.

Thomas, Sidney. "The Queen Mab Speech in *Romeo and Juliet.*" *Shakespeare Survey* 25 (1972): 73–80.

Wallace, Nathaniel. "Cultural Tropology in *Romeo and Juliet.*" *Studies in Philology* 88 (1991): 329–44.

Whittier, Gayle. "The Sonnet's Body and the Body Sonnetized in *Romeo and Juliet.*" *Shakespeare Quarterly* 40 (1989): 27–41.

Williamson, Marilyn L. "Romeo and Death." *Shakespeare Studies* 14 (1981): 129–37.

Young, Bruce W. "Haste, Consent, and Age at Marriage: Some Implications of Social History in *Romeo and Juliet.*" *Iowa State Journal of Research* 62 (1988): 459–74.

Index of
Themes and Ideas